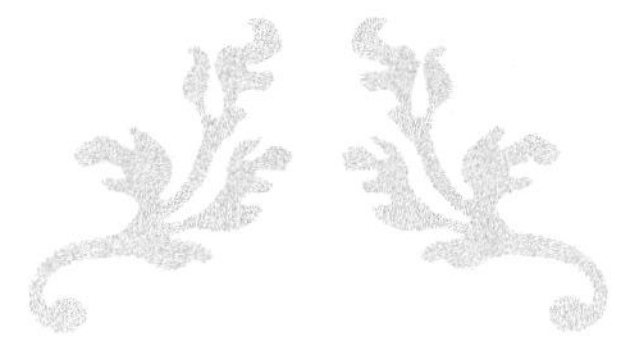

YOUTH ANXIETY AND SUBSTANCE ABUSE

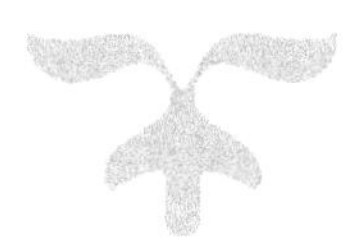

Margareth Fitzroy

Table of contents

INTRODUCTION 3

Chapter 1. Understanding Anxiety in Young people 15

Chapter 2. Lure of Substance Abuse 33

Chapter 3. The anxiety-Substance Abuse Connection 50

Chapter 4. Risk and Protective Factors 64

Chapter 5: Healthy Coping Strategies for Anxiety 77

Chapter 6: Substance Abuse Prevention and Treatment...........90

Chapter 7: Supporting Anxious Youth and Preventing Substance Abuse 104

Conclusion 111

Youth anxiety and substance abuse

<u>INTRODUCTION</u>
Overview of the Growing Problem of Anxiety and Substance Abuse Among Youth

Adolescence has long been recognized as a time of emotional turbulence and risky behavior. It's a developmental stage characterized by heightened impulsivity, sensation-seeking, and susceptibility to peer influence, as the brain undergoes rapid remodeling in preparation for adulthood (Steinberg, 2014). While some degree of emotional volatility and experimentation is considered normative, recent years have seen an explosion of more serious mental health problems among youth, namely anxiety disorders and substance abuse.

This surge cannot be dismissed as mere teenage angst or rebelliousness. Rather, it reflects a deeper crisis - one with devastating consequences for individuals, families, and society at large. According to the National Institutes of Health, nearly one in three adolescents now meets criteria for an anxiety disorder by age 18 (Merikangas et al., 2010). This represents a staggering 20% increase in just the last five years (NIH, 2018). Globally, the World Health Organization estimates that 30% of all adolescents are affected by an anxiety disorder, making it the most common mental health condition worldwide (WHO, 2019).

Comorbidity with substance abuse is alarmingly high. Over half of teens with a substance use disorder also meet diagnostic criteria for an anxiety disorder (Deas & Brown, 2006). This toxic interplay creates a vicious cycle, whereby anxious youth turn to drugs or alcohol to self-medicate their symptoms, only to find their anxiety exacerbated in the long run. Conversely, the neurological and psychological impacts of chronic substance abuse can trigger or dramatically worsen anxiety over time.

The result is a generation caught in the grip of a dual crisis. Whether it's a 14-year old popping Xanax to quell the constant hum of social anxiety, or a 20-year old shooting heroin to numb the pain of untreated PTSD, the human face of this epidemic is both heartbreaking and all too common. Walk into any high school classroom or college dorm, and you're likely to find youth struggling under the weight of crippling anxiety, compulsive substance use, or both.

The COVID-19 pandemic has only intensified this smoldering crisis. Protracted social isolation, disrupted routines, economic instability, and a constant barrage of grim headlines have sent rates of adolescent anxiety and substance abuse soaring to unprecedented levels (Leeb et al., 2020). One CDC study found that teen mental health visits to Emergency Departments skyrocketed by 31% in 2020 compared to the previous year (Yard et al., 2021). Meanwhile, suspected teen drug overdoses increased by a staggering 119% during the same period (ODMAP, 2021).

As we'll explore in depth throughout this book, the scourge of anxiety and addiction is impacting youth from all walks of life.

While certain segments of the adolescent population are at heightened risk, no group is fully immune. Upper-middle class suburban youth face many of the same mental health challenges as their less privileged urban and rural counterparts. Teenage girls tend to experience anxiety disorders at higher rates than their male peers, but the gender gap is rapidly narrowing (Bitsko et al., 2018). Across lines of race, class, culture and geography, the dual specters of anxiety and addiction have become defining features of modern adolescence.

Key Statistics on Prevalence Rates

To fully grasp the scale of this crisis, it's worth taking a deeper dive into the numbers. Let's start with anxiety disorders. According to the National Comorbidity Survey Adolescent Supplement (NCS-A), a landmark study of over 10,000 U.S. teens, a staggering 31.9% of youth meet diagnostic criteria for an anxiety disorder by age 18 (Merikangas et al., 2010). This includes Generalized Anxiety Disorder (GAD), Social Anxiety Disorder (SAD), Panic Disorder (PD), Separation Anxiety Disorder, and various phobias. Of these, Social Anxiety Disorder is the most common, affecting nearly 10% of all adolescents (NIMH, 2017).

Globally, the prevalence of adolescent anxiety disorders shows a similar pattern. A 2015 meta-analysis published in the Journal of the American Academy of Child & Adolescent Psychiatry found that 6.5% of youth worldwide had an anxiety disorder at the time of assessment, with lifetime prevalence rates exceeding 30% in some studies (Polanczyk et al., 2015). These global estimates have increased by a staggering 70% in the last 25 years alone (Lancet Commission, 2018).

Zooming in on specific anxiety disorders, the numbers are equally concerning:

- Generalized Anxiety Disorder (GAD) affects 2.2% of U.S. adolescents in a given year, with lifetime prevalence estimated at 5.7% (Merikangas et al., 2010).

- Social Anxiety Disorder (SAD) impacts nearly 10% of youth at some point before adulthood, making it the most common anxiety disorder and third most common psychiatric disorder overall in this age group (NIMH, 2017).

- Panic Disorder strikes 2-3% of teens, with onset typically occurring in late adolescence (Kessler et al., 2012).

- Separation Anxiety Disorder, once thought to be confined to childhood, is now recognized as a significant problem in adolescence as well, with lifetime prevalence rates of 7.6% (Silove et al., 2015).

Turning to substance abuse, the 2019 Monitoring the Future survey, a nationally representative study of U.S. secondary school students, found that 17% of 8th graders, 29% of 10th graders, and 36% of 12th graders had used drugs in the past year (Johnston et al., 2020). Alcohol remains the most widely abused substance, with 19% of 8th graders, 37% of 10th graders and 52% of 12th graders reporting past-year use. Meanwhile, past-year marijuana use hovers around 12%, 29% and 36% for grades 8, 10 and 12 respectively.

Particularly alarming is the skyrocketing rate of vaping among youth. Between 2017 and 2019, past-month vaping of nicotine nearly doubled in each grade, with 12% of 8th graders, 20% of 10th graders and 25% of 12th graders reporting this behavior (Johnston et al., 2020). Rates of marijuana vaping have also spiked, more than doubling among 12th graders from 7.5% in 2018 to 17% in 2019.

Globally, the United Nations Office on Drugs and Crime estimates that 35 million adolescents suffer from drug use disorders, representing a significant portion of the 247 million people who used drugs worldwide in 2018 (UNODC, 2020). Cannabis is the most commonly used illicit drug, with an estimated 188 million users globally. Opioids, including heroin and prescription painkillers, are responsible for the greatest health burden, driving an epidemic of addiction and overdose that claimed an estimated 167,000 lives in 2017 alone.

As noted earlier, comorbidity between anxiety disorders and substance abuse is the rule rather than the exception. The NCS-A study found that teens with an anxiety disorder were two to three times more likely than their non-anxious peers to develop a substance use disorder (Wolitzky-Taylor et al., 2015). Among youth with Social Anxiety Disorder, nearly half (48%) go on to develop an alcohol use disorder, while 29% develop a drug use disorder (Buckner et al., 2008).

It's a similar story with Generalized Anxiety Disorder, where 35% of affected teens abuse alcohol and 25% abuse drugs (Conway et al., 2006). For Panic Disorder, rates of alcohol and drug dependence are a staggering 63% and 60% respectively (Goodwin & Stein, 2013). In the majority of dual diagnosis cases, the anxiety disorder precedes and likely contributes to the development of substance abuse issues (NIDA, 2018).

These statistics paint a harrowing picture of a generation in crisis. With each passing year, more and more youth cross the threshold into diagnosable anxiety and addiction, only to find themselves pulled deeper into a self-perpetuating cycle of mental anguish and chemical dependency. Given the ever-increasing prevalence and devastating toll of these conditions, there has never been a more urgent need for awareness and action.

Reasons Why This Issue Needs Urgent Attention

The reasons we must treat adolescent anxiety and substance abuse as a social emergency of the highest order are both legion and gut-wrenching. First and foremost, the depths of human suffering involved are unfathomable. Anxiety disorders are characterized by relentless, often debilitating symptoms like racing thoughts, heart palpitations, nausea, dizziness, insomnia and irritability. Unchecked, these symptoms can become so severe that they interfere with basic functioning at school, work and home.

For socially anxious teens, even mundane interactions like answering a question in class, eating in the cafeteria, or navigating a conversation with peers can be a source of profound distress. Faced with constant fear of judgment, humiliation or rejection, many simply opt out, retreating into suffocating isolation. Panic attacks, which affect up to one in four anxious youth, can be particularly terrifying, often leaving the sufferer convinced they're losing their mind or literally dying (Asselmann et al., 2018).

The inner world of substance-abusing teens is often equally hellish. Caught in the grips of addiction, they find themselves consumed by an all-encompassing obsession to seek and use drugs, no matter the consequences. With inhibitions lowered and judgment impaired, they're prone to taking dangerous risks like driving under the influence, having unprotected sex, or sharing needles. Withdrawal can be a nightmarish experience, complete with intense cravings, nausea, tremors, and in severe cases, seizures or psychotic episodes (Rappeneau & Bérod, 2017).

This is to say nothing of the anguish of the parents, siblings, friends and relatives who are forced to watch helplessly as their loved one deteriorates before their eyes. Anxiety and addiction send shockwaves rippling through entire family systems, leaving a trail of strained relationships, financial hardship and emotional wreckage in their wake. Trust is shattered, dreams are dashed, and once unbreakable bonds are severed, sometimes irreparably.

Then there are the catastrophic long-term impacts on health and development. We now know that adolescence is a critical period of neurological plasticity, during which key brain regions involved in reasoning, impulse control and emotional regulation are actively under construction (Steinberg, 2014). The neural networks forged during this sensitive window lay the foundation for future mental health and overall functioning.

When this delicate process is disrupted by chronic anxiety or substance abuse, the results can be devastating. Persistent flooding of the brain with stress hormones like cortisol has been shown to cause lasting damage to the hippocampus and prefrontal cortex, impacting memory, learning, and decision-making (Sheth et al., 2017). The neurotoxic effects of drugs and alcohol can be even more severe, potentially hindering normal brain maturation and increasing susceptibility to mood disorders and cognitive impairments down the line (Chambers et al., 2019).

The toll of adolescent anxiety and addiction reverberates across every domain of functioning. Mental distress and chemical dependence wreak havoc on school performance, with affected youth more likely to have declining grades, increased absenteeism and higher dropout rates compared to their healthier peers (Brière et al., 2014). Socially, they tend to have fewer friends, more conflict with family, and a greater likelihood of being bullied or rejected by classmates (de Lijster et al., 2018).

As they transition into early adulthood, these problems often become more entrenched. Rates of unemployment, underemployment and dependence on public assistance are markedly elevated among those with adolescent-onset anxiety and substance use disorders (Mojtabai et al., 2015). They're also more prone to legal troubles, accidental injury and intimate partner violence (Davis et al., 2020). Most tragically, their risk of premature death – whether by suicide, overdose or other preventable causes – is heartbreakingly high (Whiteford et al., 2015).

If the incalculable human costs alone weren't enough to classify this crisis as a top-level emergency, then the dollars and cents surely clinch it. According to the World Economic Forum, mental disorders are on track to cost the global economy a staggering $16 trillion in lost output by 2030, making them the single largest drain on economic productivity (Bloom et al., 2012). Anxiety disorders and substance abuse will account for a significant chunk of these losses, to the tune of $2.5 trillion and $1.5 trillion respectively (Lancet Commission, 2018).

When you factor in the towering direct costs of treatment, criminal justice involvement, social services and other collateral damage, the total economic burden is positively mind-boggling. In the U.S. alone, the yearly tab for adolescent mental disorders exceeds $250 billion, while substance abuse costs upwards of $450 billion annually (National Research Council, 2009; NIDA, 2017). For perspective, that's more than the GDP of entire developed nations like Norway, Ireland or Israel.

Then there's the opportunity cost to consider – the immeasurable waste of human potential that occurs when promising young minds are derailed by mental illness and addiction. How many budding artists, entrepreneurs, scientists and leaders has our society been robbed of because we failed to intervene in time? What groundbreaking innovations and creative marvels might we have enjoyed if more of our youth were empowered to thrive? The loss is unfathomable.

Ultimately, there is no facet of society that goes untouched by this crisis. The pain is personal, the costs communal. With each day we fail to act, we hemorrhage resources – both human and economic – on an unimaginable scale. The ripple effects span generations, robbing individuals of productive, fulfilling lives while eroding the very bedrock of our communities. This is, by any metric, an all-hands-on-deck emergency.

Yet for far too long, a toxic combination of stigma, misinformation and systemic neglect has allowed this slow-motion catastrophe to metastasize largely unabated. Anxious and addicted youth have been relegated to the shadows, their struggles dismissed as signs of personal weakness rather than symptoms of a societal ill. Even when their distress could no longer be ignored, they've had to navigate a fragmented, underfunded and often unresponsive treatment landscape, with heartbreaking consequences.

It's long past time we as a society summoned the courage to confront this crisis head-on. With rates of adolescent anxiety and addiction climbing by the day, and with an entire generation's wellbeing hanging in the balance, we can't afford to wait a moment longer. The human and economic costs are simply too great. It's time to sound the alarm from the rooftops.

Make no mistake, there are no quick fixes here. Tackling a challenge of this magnitude will require a full-scale societal mobilization, on par with the resolute unity of purpose we've mustered to confront existential threats like war or environmental catastrophe. We need all hands on deck – policymakers, mental health professionals, educators, parents, and youth themselves working in lockstep to implement bold, evidence-based solutions.

The good news is, we already have many of the tools we need to begin turning the tide. From cutting-edge therapeutic interventions to school- and community-based prevention programs, there's a growing arsenal of weapons at our disposal in the fight against adolescent anxiety and addiction. What's been missing is the political will and societal resolve to take this fight to the next level – to make adolescent mental health a top-tier priority and to back that commitment up with serious resources.

Throughout the rest of this book, we'll take a deep dive into the programs and policies that are already making a difference, as well as those that hold the greatest promise for transformative change. We'll also grapple honestly with the entrenched obstacles that have allowed this crisis to fester for so long, from the stigma surrounding mental illness to the fragmentation of our behavioral health system.

But make no mistake, this is ultimately a book about hope. Because as daunting as the challenge before us may seem, there is ample reason for optimism. We find ourselves at a unique inflection point, with a historic opportunity to reimagine how we support adolescent mental health in this country. From surging public awareness to breakthrough scientific insights to mounting bipartisan momentum for reform, the stars are aligning for transformative progress.

The only question is whether we'll seize this moment. Will we find the courage to confront this crisis with the urgency and resolve it so clearly demands? Will we harness the immense talents and energies of this rising generation, or allow them to be squandered by the phantoms of anxiety and addiction?

Our answer to these questions will reverberate for generations to come. Because in the final analysis, there is no challenge more critical – no cause more consequential – than ensuring the health and flourishing of our youth. They are our future. Now let's fight like it.

Chapter 1. Understanding Anxiety in Young people

Common Types of Anxiety Disorders in Youth

Anxiety disorders are the most common mental health conditions affecting young people today, with nearly one in three adolescents meeting diagnostic criteria for an anxiety disorder by the age of 18 (Merikangas et al., 2010). While the experience of anxiety can vary significantly from person to person, there are several distinct types of anxiety disorders that tend to emerge during the teenage years. Understanding the unique features and manifestations of each can be an important first step in identifying and addressing problematic anxiety in youth.

Generalized Anxiety Disorder (GAD) is one of the most prevalent anxiety disorders, impacting anywhere from 2-5% of children and adolescents (NIMH, 2020). Youth with GAD experience excessive, uncontrollable worry about a wide range of topics, from their performance at school to their family's financial status to potential catastrophes on the news. They may find themselves caught in an endless loop of "what if" thinking, perpetually bracing for worst-case scenarios in multiple domains of life.

This pervasive sense of dread is often accompanied by physical symptoms like muscle tension, headaches, restlessness, difficulty concentrating, and sleep disturbances (Ruscio & Khazanov, 2017). To meet diagnostic criteria for GAD, symptoms must occur more days than not for at least six months and cause significant distress or impairment in daily functioning (American Psychiatric Association, 2013).

Social Anxiety Disorder (SAD), sometimes referred to as social phobia, is another common anxiety disorder that typically first emerges in the early to mid-teen years (NIMH, 2020). Youth with SAD have an intense, persistent fear of social situations, particularly those that involve being observed, evaluated or judged by others. This could include everything from speaking up in class to attending parties to ordering food at a restaurant.

At the heart of social anxiety is an overwhelming fear of embarrassing oneself or doing something to elicit rejection, ridicule or disapproval from others. Physical symptoms like blushing, trembling, sweating and nausea are common in feared social situations, as are racing thoughts and a powerful urge to escape (Masia Warner et al., 2016). In severe cases, youth may go to great lengths to avoid anxiety-provoking social encounters altogether, leading to increasing isolation and withdrawal.

Panic Disorder, while less common than GAD or SAD, is a potentially debilitating condition that affects roughly 2-3% of adolescents (Kessler et al., 2012). It is characterized by recurrent, unexpected panic attacks – abrupt surges of intense fear or discomfort that peak within minutes and are accompanied by a range of frightening physical sensations like heart palpitations, shortness of breath, dizziness and depersonalization (the feeling of being detached from one's body).

Youth with Panic Disorder often develop a paralyzing fear of having additional attacks, to the point where they significantly alter their behavior in an attempt to prevent them. They may avoid specific places or situations that they associate with past attacks, like crowded spaces or public transportation. In some cases, their world may narrow to the confines of home, as venturing beyond feels too risky. Many become hyper-attuned to benign changes in their body, misinterpreting normal fluctuations in heart rate or breathing as signs of impending catastrophe (Raffa et al., 2018).

Separation Anxiety Disorder, while more commonly diagnosed in younger children, can also affect adolescents and even adults. It involves an excessive, persistent fear of being apart from one's primary attachment figures, whether that's a parent, caregiver or even an older sibling (Silove & Rees, 2014). Youth with Separation Anxiety Disorder may worry incessantly about their loved ones being harmed or may have difficulty sleeping alone, attending school or engaging in other normative activities that require separation.

Physical complaints like headaches, nausea or fatigue are common on school days or in other situations that involve being apart from attachment figures. In some cases, youth may resort to pleading, tantrums or even threats of self-harm to avoid separation (Wehry et al., 2015). While a certain degree of separation anxiety is developmentally appropriate in early childhood, persistence of these symptoms into the teen years can lead to significant functional impairment.

Finally, various Specific Phobias – intense, irrational fears of specific objects or situations – are also common in youth. These might include phobias of animals (e.g. dogs, snakes, insects), natural environments (e.g. heights, storms, water), blood-injection-injury (e.g. needles, medical procedures), or other specific situations (e.g. flying, driving, choking). When exposed to the feared stimulus, youth with specific phobias may experience immediate, intense anxiety along with physical symptoms like increased heart rate, shortness of breath and trembling (Cornacchio et al., 2019).

While many youth have mild, transient fears that don't cause significant impairment, for those with full-blown phobias, even the mere anticipation of encountering the feared object or situation can be immensely distressing. They may go to great lengths to avoid triggers, rearranging their lives in ways that can interfere with academic, social or recreational functioning (Wardenaar et al., 2017).

It's important to note that it's possible, and in fact quite common, for youth to meet diagnostic criteria for multiple anxiety disorders simultaneously. Roughly 40% of anxious adolescents have more than one anxiety disorder, with GAD and SAD being the most frequent combination (NIMH, 2020). Comorbidity with depression is also extremely high, occurring in up to 60% of anxious youth (Essau et al., 2014). When multiple disorders co-occur, symptoms tend to be more severe and impairing, highlighting the importance of comprehensive assessment and multimodal treatment.

Symptoms and Diagnostic Criteria

While the specific symptoms of anxiety can vary depending on the particular disorder, there are some common signs and features that cut across diagnostic categories. At the broadest level, pathological anxiety involves excessive fear or worry that is persistent, difficult to control, and out of proportion to the actual threat posed by a situation (American Psychiatric Association, 2013). This anxiety is often accompanied by a range of physical symptoms, cognitive symptoms and behavioral manifestations.

Physical symptoms are often among the most readily observable signs of an anxiety disorder in youth. These may include (Ramsawh et al., 2014; Siegel & Dickstein, 2012):

• Muscle tension, trembling or shaking

• Restlessness, fidgeting or difficulty sitting still

• Rapid heartbeat or heart palpitations

• Shortness of breath or difficulty breathing

• Sweating, flushing or chills

• Dizziness or lightheadedness

• Nausea, vomiting or abdominal pain

• Numbness or tingling sensations in the extremities

• Insomnia or other sleep disturbances

• Fatigue or low energy

Importantly, the presence of these physical symptoms alone does not necessarily indicate an anxiety disorder, as many can also occur in the context of other medical conditions or even in response to normative stress. However, when multiple physical symptoms co-occur and are accompanied by excessive worry or avoidance behaviors, an anxiety disorder becomes more likely.

Cognitive symptoms refer to the worrisome thoughts, beliefs and expectations that fuel and maintain anxiety. These may include (Castagna et al., 2018; Masi et al., 2020):

- Pervasive, uncontrollable worry about multiple life domains

- Persistent thoughts about worst-case scenarios or catastrophic outcomes

- Difficulty concentrating, mind going "blank" or racing thoughts

- Rumination (repetitively going over anxious thoughts or problems)

- Overestimation of the likelihood or severity of feared outcomes

- Rigid or inflexible thinking patterns (e.g. "if I make one mistake, it will be a disaster")

- Intolerance of uncertainty or ambiguity

- Hypervigilance or a chronic sense of being "on edge"

- Fear of losing control or "going crazy"

- Worry about the judgment or evaluation of others

These maladaptive thoughts and beliefs are a key factor in perpetuating anxiety, as they lead youth to interpret even benign or ambiguous situations as threatening. Over time, these cognitive distortions can become so automatic and ingrained that youth may not even be fully aware of them. One of the primary goals of cognitive-behavioral therapy (CBT), the gold standard psychotherapy for anxiety disorders, is to help youth identify and challenge these distorted thoughts.

Finally, anxiety disorders are associated with a range of behavioral symptoms that can significantly interfere with daily functioning. These may include (Creswell et al., 2015; Swan et al., 2016):

• Avoidance of feared objects, situations or activities

•• Avoidance of feared objects, situations or activities

• Escape or flight from anxiety-provoking situations

• Excessive reassurance-seeking from parents, teachers or peers

• Compulsive safety behaviors (e.g. checking, washing, ordering, counting)

• Procrastination or avoidance of important tasks

• Decline in academic performance or school attendance

• Withdrawal from social interactions or relationships

• Substance use as a means of coping with anxiety

• Angry outbursts or irritability when feeling anxious

• Overdependence on parents or caregivers

These avoidance and safety behaviors are often highly reinforcing in the short-term, as they provide immediate relief from anxiety. However, in the long run, they prevent youth from learning that their feared outcomes are unlikely to occur and that they are capable of coping with anxiety-provoking situations. This maintains and exacerbates the anxiety over time. Treatment often involves gradual exposure to feared stimuli and situations, with the goal of building tolerance and confidence.

To meet diagnostic criteria for an anxiety disorder, a youth's symptoms must not only be excessive and impairing, but must also be persistent. For most anxiety disorders, symptoms must be present for at least several months and must occur more days than not (American Psychiatric Association, 2013). Furthermore, the symptoms must cause clinically significant distress or impairment in social, academic, occupational or other important areas of functioning.

It's important to note that many anxious youth, particularly those with GAD, may not exhibit obvious behavioral symptoms like avoidance or escape. Instead, their anxiety may manifest primarily through physical symptoms, excessive worry and internal distress (Hoffman & Mathew, 2008). This can make detection more challenging, as these "invisible" symptoms are easily overlooked by parents, teachers and even clinicians.

Assessment of anxiety disorders typically involves a multi-method, multi-informant approach. Structured diagnostic interviews like the Anxiety Disorders Interview Schedule for Children (ADIS-C) are considered the gold standard, but self-report questionnaires, parent and teacher rating scales, and behavioral observations can also provide valuable information (Silverman & Ollendick, 2005). Given the high rates of comorbidity among anxiety disorders and with other conditions like depression, a comprehensive assessment should screen for a range of potential diagnoses.

Developmental Factors That Make Youth Vulnerable to Anxiety

Adolescence is a unique developmental stage characterized by rapid physical, cognitive, social and emotional changes. While this period of growth and exploration can be exciting, it can also be destabilizing, as youth navigate new challenges and expectations with an still-maturing repertoire of coping skills. Several key features of adolescent development may make youth particularly vulnerable to anxiety during this time.

From a neurobiological perspective, adolescence is marked by significant changes in brain structure and function. The limbic system, which is involved in processing emotions and rewards, matures relatively early and is thought to be hypersensitive during the teen years (Ernst et al., 2005). In contrast, the prefrontal cortex, which is responsible for executive functions like planning, decision-making and impulse control, continues to develop well into the 20s (Giedd, 2015).

This "mismatch" in the maturation of emotional and cognitive control systems may predispose adolescents to experience emotions, including anxiety, more intensely, while simultaneously limiting their capacity to regulate those emotions effectively (Crone & Dahl, 2012). This could explain why anxiety disorders so often emerge during the teenage years, as youth struggle to cope with developmentally normative stressors using a still-developing toolkit of cognitive and emotional regulation skills.

Psychosocial factors also play a significant role. Adolescence is a time of increasing autonomy, as youth begin to individuate from their families and forge their own identities. This can be an anxiety-provoking process, as it involves greater exposure to novel and potentially challenging situations, from academic pressures to social dynamics to romantic relationships (Blakemore & Mills, 2014). At the same time, adolescents become increasingly self-conscious and attuned to the perceptions of their peers, which can fuel social anxiety.

Modern technology may further exacerbate these vulnerabilities. The advent of social media has created a virtual fishbowl in which youth are constantly curating their image and seeking validation from their peers (Twenge, 2019). This 24/7 connectivity can amplify the fear of missing out (FOMO) and make even minor social slights feel devastating. Cyberbullying, which is experienced by up to a third of teens, can also be a potent trigger for anxiety and related concerns (Nixon, 2014).

From an evolutionary perspective, some degree of anxiety is adaptive, as it helps us detect and respond to potential threats.

However, in today's relatively safe environments, these threat-detection systems can become overactive, leading to false alarms and excessive anxiety (Bateson et al., 2011). This may be especially true for modern adolescents, who have grown up in an era of global terrorism, school shootings, climate change and now, a viral pandemic. This chronic sense of background threat, amplified by 24-hour news and social media, could be priming youth to be more anxious.

Family and parenting factors also shape vulnerability to anxiety. Children of anxious parents are up to seven times more likely to develop an anxiety disorder themselves, through a combination of genetic and environmental influences (Drake & Ginsburg, 2012). Parenting styles characterized by overprotection, intrusiveness, and excessive accommodation of anxious behaviors can inadvertently reinforce anxiety by depriving youth of opportunities to develop autonomy and coping skills (Griffith et al., 2020).

Conversely, authoritarian parenting styles marked by high expectations and low warmth have also been linked to increased anxiety in youth (Gecas & Seff, 1990). Family stress, conflict and dysfunction more broadly have been identified as risk factors for anxiety disorders (McCauley Ohannessian, 2014). Importantly, these family factors interact with individual characteristics like temperament and cognitive style to shape anxiety risk.

Finally, certain temperamental and cognitive factors may make some youth more susceptible to anxiety than others. Youth who are behaviorally inhibited – characterized by shyness, fearfulness and withdrawal in novel situations – are at increased risk for developing anxiety disorders (Sandstrom et al., 2020). Perfectionistic tendencies, excessive need for control, intolerance of uncertainty and anxiety sensitivity (fear of anxiety-related sensations) have also been identified as cognitive risk factors (Newton & Castonguay, 2013).

Youth with these predisposing factors may be more likely to perceive situations as threatening, to catastrophize about potential negative outcomes, and to doubt their ability to cope – all cognitive processes that fuel anxiety. Importantly, these cognitive styles are not fixed traits, but learned patterns of thinking that can be modified through targeted interventions like cognitive-behavioral therapy (CBT).

Impact of Anxiety on Mental Health, Academic Performance, Relationships

Anxiety disorders can have a profound and pervasive impact on youth functioning, interfering with their ability to learn, grow and thrive during this critical developmental period. When left untreated, anxiety can set youth on a trajectory of ongoing mental health problems, academic difficulties and interpersonal challenges that can reverberate well into adulthood.

One of the most immediate impacts of anxiety is on youth mental health. Anxious youth are at significantly increased risk for developing comorbid depression, with rates of co-occurrence ranging from 10-50% (Wolk et al., 2016). This comorbidity is associated with greater symptom severity, functional impairment and suicidality compared to either disorder alone (Melton et al., 2016). Anxiety has also been identified as a risk factor for the development of substance use disorders, as youth may turn to drugs or alcohol to cope with overwhelming anxiety symptoms (Blumenthal et al., 2019).

The chronic stress of living with an untreated anxiety disorder can also take a toll on physical health. Anxiety has been linked to a range of somatic symptoms and conditions, from headaches and gastrointestinal problems to cardiovascular disease and weakened immune function (Culpepper, 2009). The persistent hyperarousal associated with anxiety disorders can lead to changes in stress response systems that have long-term implications for health and disease (McEwen, 2012).

Academically, anxiety can significantly interfere with learning and performance. Youth with anxiety disorders are more likely to struggle with concentration, memory and test performance, leading to lower grades and academic achievement (Kessler et al., 2014). Excessive worry and rumination can make it difficult for anxious youth to focus on lectures or complete assignments in a timely manner. Procrastination and avoidance of challenging tasks is common, further compounding academic difficulties (Waite et al., 2021).

In severe cases, anxiety can lead to school refusal, where youth experience such intense distress about attending school that they are unable to go for an extended period. Up to 5% of school-aged children experience problematic school refusal, and anxiety disorders are the most common underlying cause (Ek & Eriksson, 2013). The academic consequences of chronic absenteeism can be severe, including falling behind in coursework, reduced educational attainment, and increased risk of dropout (Attwood & Croll, 2015).

Socially, anxiety disorders can significantly impair youth's ability to form and maintain relationships. Social anxiety in particular can make it challenging for youth to initiate conversations, join group activities, or assert their needs in interpersonal situations (Miers et al., 2014). Fear of negative evaluation by peers may lead anxious youth to avoid social situations altogether, leading to isolation and loneliness.

Even when they do engage in social interactions, anxious youth may have difficulty truly connecting with others, as their attention is often internally focused on their own anxiety symptoms and worries (Haller et al., 2014). This self-focus can make them appear disinterested or aloof, further impeding social success. Over time, these social difficulties can lead to peer rejection, victimization and a negative social reputation that can be difficult to shake (Kingery et al., 2010).

Within the family system, child anxiety can strain parent-child relationships and family functioning. Parents may become frustrated with their child's avoidance behaviors or excessive reassurance-seeking, leading to conflict and reduced warmth in the relationship (Lebowitz et al., 2012). Anxious youth may also have difficulty individuating from their parents, leading to overdependence and reduced autonomy development (Rubin et al., 2009).

In some cases, parents may accommodate their child's anxiety in an attempt to reduce distress, such as allowing them to avoid feared situations or providing excessive reassurance. While well-intentioned, these accommodations can inadvertently reinforce the child's anxiety in the long-term (Lebowitz et al., 2014). The stress of parenting an anxious child can also take a toll on parental mental health and marital satisfaction (Teetsel et al., 2014).

If left untreated, the impacts of anxiety in adolescence can persist and even intensify into adulthood. Longitudinal studies have shown that youth with anxiety disorders are at increased risk for a range of adverse outcomes in adulthood, including:

• Anxiety and depressive disorders (Lin et al., 2020)

• Substance abuse and dependence (Wolitzky-Taylor et al., 2015)

• Suicidal ideation and attempts (Wunderlich et al., 1998)

• Lower educational attainment (Van Ameringen et al., 2003)

• Reduced occupational functioning (Moitra et al., 2011)

• Relationship problems and reduced life satisfaction (Essau et al., 2014)

Importantly, receiving effective treatment for anxiety during the critical period of adolescence can alter these trajectories and improve long-term outcomes. Youth who receive cognitive-behavioral therapy (CBT), the gold-standard psychotherapy for anxiety disorders, show significant reductions in anxiety symptoms that are maintained years after treatment (Kendall et al., 2016). Early intervention may prevent the development of comorbid disorders and the entrenchment of maladaptive coping patterns that can make anxiety more resistant to treatment over time.

Beyond symptom reduction, treatment can also have ripple effects across multiple domains of functioning. Youth who overcome their anxiety are better able to engage in the academic and social experiences that are crucial for healthy development. They are more likely to form close friendships, participate in extracurricular activities, and take on new challenges that build self-efficacy and resilience (Swan & Kendall, 2016). Within the family system, reduced child anxiety can lead to improved parent-child relationships and overall family functioning (Wood et al., 2003).

Given the high prevalence and significant impact of anxiety disorders in youth, there is a critical need for increased awareness, early identification and access to evidence-based treatments. Schools, as a near-universal point of contact for youth, are uniquely positioned to play a key role in this process. School-based mental health screening can help identify anxious youth who may otherwise go undetected and connect them with services (Cuijpers et al., 2008).

Training teachers and other school staff to recognize signs of anxiety can also improve early identification and referral to treatment (Osher et al., 2014). Integrating mental health education into the curriculum can help destigmatize anxiety and teach youth strategies for managing stress and worries (Werner-

Seidler et al., 2019). For youth with mild to moderate anxiety, school-based group CBT interventions have been shown to be effective in reducing symptoms (Mychailyszyn et al., 2012).

At a societal level, increasing access to affordable, evidence-based mental health services is crucial. Despite the existence of effective treatments, only a minority of anxious youth receive the care they need (Chavira et al., 2017). Barriers to treatment are numerous, including stigma, lack of mental health literacy, insufficient provider availability, and financial constraints (Reardon et al., 2017). Addressing these barriers will require a coordinated effort across healthcare, education and policy sectors.

Promising directions include integrating behavioral health services into primary care settings, leveraging technology to deliver interventions, and implementing policies that mandate insurance coverage for mental health on par with physical health (Triana et al., 2019). Investing in the mental health of our youth is not only a moral imperative, but also a sound economic strategy, as the societal costs of untreated anxiety disorders are immense (Konnopka et al., 2012).

In conclusion, anxiety disorders in youth represent a significant public health concern with far-reaching impacts on mental health, academic functioning, social relationships and long-term trajectories. The unique developmental challenges of adolescence, coupled with the rapidly changing social and technological landscape, may be contributing to rising rates of anxiety in this population.

However, we are not powerless in the face of this epidemic. With greater awareness, early intervention and expanded access to evidence-based treatments, we can change the course for anxious youth and set them on a path to thriving. This will require a collective commitment from parents, educators, healthcare providers, researchers and policymakers to prioritize the mental health of our youth. The stakes could not be higher, as the well-being of an entire generation hangs in the balance.

Chapter 2. Lure of Substance Abuse

Most Commonly Abused Substances Among Youth

Substance abuse among adolescents and young adults is a significant public health concern, with far-reaching consequences for individual health, social functioning, and societal costs. While the landscape of substance use is constantly evolving, with new drugs emerging and patterns of use shifting over time, certain substances have consistently been among the most commonly abused by youth. Understanding the prevalence, effects, and appeal of these substances is a crucial first step in developing targeted prevention and intervention strategies.

Alcohol is by far the most widely used substance among youth, with nearly 60% of 12th graders reporting having consumed alcohol at some point in their lives (Johnston et al., 2021). While rates of binge drinking (defined as consuming five or more drinks in a row) have declined in recent years, it remains a significant problem, with 16% of 12th graders reporting binge drinking in the past two weeks (Johnston et al., 2021). The widespread availability of alcohol, coupled with its central role in many social and cultural contexts, contributes to its high rates of use among youth.

Marijuana is the most commonly used illicit drug among adolescents, with 35% of 12th graders reporting having used marijuana in the past year (Johnston et al., 2021). The perceived risk associated with marijuana use has decreased significantly over the past decade, likely due in part to the legalization of marijuana for medical and recreational use in many states (Miech et al., 2021). This shift in attitudes, along with increasing potency of marijuana products, is concerning given the potential impacts of marijuana on the developing brain.

Nicotine, traditionally delivered through combustible cigarettes, has long been one of the most commonly used substances among youth. However, the landscape of nicotine use has changed dramatically in recent years with the emergence of electronic cigarettes, or e-cigarettes. E-cigarette use, also known as vaping, has surged among youth, with 22% of 12th graders reporting vaping nicotine in the past 30 days (Johnston et al., 2021). The appealing flavors, sleek design, and perceived safety of e-cigarettes have contributed to their popularity among youth, despite growing evidence of their health risks.

Prescription drugs, particularly opioid pain relievers, stimulants prescribed for attention-deficit/hyperactivity disorder (ADHD), and central nervous system (CNS) depressants used for anxiety and sleep disorders, are also commonly misused by youth. In 2020, 5% of 12th graders reported misusing prescription opioids in the past year, while 6% reported misusing prescription stimulants (Johnston et al., 2021). The widespread availability of these medications, coupled with the misconception that they are safe because they are prescribed by doctors, has contributed to their abuse among youth.

Other substances commonly used by youth include synthetic cannabinoids (known as K2 or Spice), which are human-made chemicals that produce effects similar to those of marijuana;

inhalants, which are volatile substances that produce chemical vapors that can be inhaled to induce a psychoactive effect; and hallucinogens like LSD, psilocybin mushrooms, and salvia (Johnston et al., 2021). While the use of these substances is less prevalent than alcohol, marijuana, nicotine, and prescription drugs, they still pose significant risks to the health and well-being of youth.

It's important to note that polysubstance use, or the use of multiple substances, is common among youth. In 2020, 19% of 12th graders reported using two or more substances in the past year (Johnston et al., 2021). Polysubstance use is associated with increased risks of adverse health outcomes, including overdose, as well as mental health problems and addiction (Hassan et al., 2020).

The patterns and prevalence of substance use among youth are not uniform across all demographic groups. Males are more likely than females to use most substances, although this gender gap has narrowed in recent years (Johnston et al., 2021). Rates of substance use also vary by race/ethnicity, with white youth generally having the highest rates of use for most substances (Johnston et al., 2021). However, these racial/ethnic differences are complex and often intersect with other factors like socioeconomic status, family structure, and community influences.

Reasons Young People Turn to Drugs and Alcohol

Adolescence is a period of significant developmental changes, marked by a complex interplay of biological, psychological, and social factors. This unique confluence of influences can make youth particularly vulnerable to substance use and its consequences. Understanding the reasons why young people turn to drugs and alcohol is essential for developing effective prevention and intervention strategies.

One of the most powerful influences on youth substance use is peer pressure. During adolescence, the desire for social acceptance and fear of rejection are at their peak (Blakemore & Mills, 2014). Youth may feel compelled to use substances to fit in with their peer group, especially if substance use is seen as normative or socially desirable within that group (Simons-Morton & Chen, 2006). Peer influence can operate directly, through overt offers or encouragement to use substances, or indirectly, through modeling of substance use behaviors and shaping of norms and expectations (Wood et al., 2004).

The developmental drive for novelty and sensation-seeking is another factor that can contribute to youth substance use. Adolescence is characterized by an increased sensitivity to reward and a decreased sensitivity to risk, which can lead to impulsive and risky decision-making (Steinberg, 2010). Substances can be appealing to youth because they offer novel, exciting experiences and intense sensations. This drive for novelty and excitement can overpower the still-developing capacity for self-regulation and impulse control (Somerville et al., 2010).

For many youth, substance use serves as a means of self-medication for underlying mental health problems. Anxiety, depression, trauma, and stress are all common in adolescence, and youth may turn to substances as a way to cope with these challenges (Wills & Filer, 1996). Substances can provide temporary relief from psychological distress, but over time, this pattern of self-medication can lead to the development of substance use disorders and exacerbate mental health problems (Swendsen et al., 2010).

The desire for autonomy and rebellion against authority is another developmental factor that can contribute to youth substance use. As adolescents strive to establish their independence and identity, they may resist or rebel against parental and societal norms (Ellis, 2003). Substance use can be seen as a way to assert autonomy, defy authority figures, and differentiate oneself from the expectations of family and society (Dawson & Carr, 2009).

Experimentation and curiosity are normal parts of adolescent development, and for many youth, substance use is a way to satisfy this curiosity (Shedler & Block, 1990). The desire to experience new sensations, altered states of consciousness, and the unknown can be powerful motivators for trying substances. The perception that "everyone is doing it" can also fuel curiosity and experimentation, as youth may feel they are missing out on a common experience (Sanders, 2013).

Family factors play a significant role in shaping youth substance use. Parental substance use, favorable parental attitudes towards substance use, and lack of parental monitoring are all associated with increased risk of substance use among youth (Hawkins et al., 1992). Conversely, strong family bonds, clear family rules and expectations regarding substance use, and parental involvement and support are protective factors that can reduce the likelihood of youth substance use (Haggerty et al., 2013).

The availability and accessibility of substances in a youth's environment can also influence their likelihood of use. When drugs and alcohol are easily obtainable, either through peers, family members, or the community, youth are more likely to use them (Keyes et al., 2012). The perception that substances are readily available can also increase use, even if actual availability is limited (Stanley et al., 2006).

Media and popular culture can also shape youth attitudes and norms around substance use. Depictions of substance use in movies, television shows, music, and social media can normalize and glamorize these behaviors, especially when portrayed by celebrities or characters admired by youth (Morgenstern et al., 2011). Alcohol and tobacco advertising, which often targets youth with appealing imagery and themes of fun, social success, and rebellion, can also influence youth perceptions of these substances (Anderson et al., 2009).

Finally, broader societal and cultural factors can shape youth substance use. Socioeconomic disadvantage, community disorganization, and lack of opportunities for prosocial involvement are all associated with increased risk of youth substance use (Arthur et al., 2002). Cultural norms and attitudes regarding substance use, which can vary widely across communities and subgroups, can also influence youth behaviors (Morrow et al., 2006).

Understanding the complex web of influences that can lead youth to use substances is crucial for developing comprehensive, multi-level prevention and interventionstrategies. These strategies must address not only the individual factors that make youth vulnerable to substance use, but also the peer, family, community, and societal influences that shape youth attitudes and behaviors.

Short-Term vs Long-Term Effects of Substance Use on the Developing Brain

Adolescence is a critical period of brain development, marked by significant changes in brain structure, function, and connectivity. The brain does not fully mature until the mid-20s, with the prefrontal cortex, which is responsible for executive functions like decision-making, impulse control, and planning, being one of the last areas to develop (Giedd, 2015). This ongoing development makes the adolescent brain particularly vulnerable to the effects of substance use.

The short-term effects of substance use on the brain can vary depending on the specific substance, the amount used, and the individual. Alcohol, for example, is a central nervous system depressant that can cause slurred speech, impaired memory and coordination, slowed reaction times, and altered perceptions and emotions (Squeglia et al., 2014). Marijuana can cause acute effects like altered senses, changes in mood, impaired memory and problem-solving, and delusions or hallucinations (van Ours & Williams, 2012). Nicotine, a stimulant, can cause increased alertness, attention, and memory, as well as reduced appetite and anxiety in the short-term (Kota et al., 2007).

While these acute effects are often the reason youth seek out substances, they can also lead to dangerous consequences. The impairments in judgment, coordination, and reaction time caused by alcohol and other substances can lead to accidents, injuries, and risky behaviors like unprotected sex and driving under the influence (Hingson et al., 2009). The altered perceptions and emotions caused by substances can also lead to aggressiveness, violence, and other problematic behaviors (Boles & Miotto, 2003).

Even more concerning are the long-term effects of substance use on the developing brain. Chronic substance use during adolescence can lead to structural and functional changes in the brain that can have lasting consequences for cognitive, emotional, and social functioning.

Alcohol, for example, can cause damage to the hippocampus, a brain region crucial for memory and learning (McClain et al., 2011). Chronic alcohol use during adolescence has been associated with reduced hippocampal volume, which can lead to deficits in verbal and nonverbal memory (Medina et al., 2007). Alcohol can also damage the prefrontal cortex, leading to problems with executive functioning, decision-making, and impulse control that can persist into adulthood (Squeglia et al., 2014).

Marijuana use during adolescence has been associated with changes in brain structure and function, particularly in areas involved in memory, learning, and impulse control. Regular marijuana use during the teen years has been linked to lower IQ scores in adulthood, even after stopping use (Meier et al., 2012). Marijuana use has also been associated with changes in the brain's reward system, which can increase the likelihood of addiction to other substances (Koob & Volkow, 2016).

Nicotine exposure during adolescence can have lasting effects on brain development and functioning. The adolescent brain is particularly sensitive to the effects of nicotine, with exposure leading to long-term changes in the brain's reward and stress systems (Yuan et al., 2015). These changes can make youth more vulnerable to addiction to nicotine and other substances later in life (Leslie, 2020).

Stimulants like amphetamines and cocaine can cause significant changes in brain chemistry and structure when used during adolescence. Chronic stimulant use has been associated with reduced gray matter in the prefrontal cortex, which can lead to problems with decision-making, impulse control, and emotion regulation (Singer et al., 2002). Stimulant use can also cause long-term changes in the brain's dopamine system, which is involved in reward and motivation (Volkow et al., 2011).

The long-term effects of substance use on the brain can translate into significant consequences for mental health and behavior. Substance use during adolescence is associated with increased risk of developing substance use disorders, as well as other mental health problems like depression, anxiety, and psychosis (Choi et al., 2017). The cognitive deficits caused by substance use, such as problems with memory, attention, and decision-making, can also interfere with academic performance and occupational functioning (Jacobus et al., 2009).

It's important to note that the effects of substance use on the developing brain can be influenced by a variety of factors, including the age of onset of use, the frequency and quantity of use, and individual genetic and environmental factors. Some youth may be more vulnerable to the effects of substances due to pre-existing mental health problems, family history of substance use, or other risk factors (Chambers et al., 2015).

The good news is that the adolescent brain, while vulnerable, is also remarkably plastic and capable of recovery. Stopping substance use, especially early in adolescence, can allow the brain to recover and can prevent many of the long-term consequences (Chung et al., 2014). However, the longer substance use continues, the more difficult it can be to reverse the changes in brain structure and function (Brown et al., 2013).

This underscores the importance of early intervention and prevention efforts. Educating youth about the risks of substance use, providing skills for coping with stress and peer pressure, and creating environments that discourage substance use can all help prevent the initiation of use and the development of substance use disorders (Stone et al., 2012). For youth who have already begun using substances, early intervention and treatment can help prevent the progression to more serious use and can mitigate the long-term effects on the brain (Winters et al., 2007).

Substance Use Disorders - Signs and Symptoms

Substance use disorders (SUDs) are characterized by a problematic pattern of substance use that leads to significant impairment or distress. SUDs exist on a continuum, ranging from mild to severe, and can involve any type of substance, including alcohol, tobacco, marijuana, prescription drugs, and illicit drugs.

The Diagnostic and Statistical Manual of Mental Disorders, Fifth Edition (DSM-5), which is used by mental health professionals to diagnose mental disorders, defines SUDs based on a set of 11 criteria (American Psychiatric Association, 2013). These criteria fall into four main categories: impaired control, social impairment, risky use, and pharmacological criteria (tolerance and withdrawal).

Impaired control refers to the inability to reduce or control substance use despite a desire to do so. This can manifest as using larger amounts of the substance or using for a longer period than intended, spending a great deal of time obtaining, using, or recovering from the substance, and having cravings or a strong desire to use the substance (APA, 2013).

Social impairment involves the failure to fulfill major role obligations at work, school, or home due to substance use, continued use despite persistent or recurrent social or interpersonal problems caused or exacerbated by the substance, and giving up or reducing important social, occupational, or recreational activities because of substance use (APA, 2013).

Risky use encompasses the recurrent use of the substance in situations where it is physically hazardous, such as driving while impaired, and continued use despite knowledge of a persistent or recurrent physical or psychological problem that is likely to have been caused or exacerbated by the substance (APA, 2013).

The pharmacological criteria include tolerance, which is the need for markedly increased amounts of the substance to achieve the desired effect or a markedly diminished effect with continued use of the same amount, and withdrawal, which is a characteristic syndrome that occurs when blood or tissue concentrations of a substance decline in an individual who had maintained prolonged heavy use of the substance (APA, 2013).

The severity of an SUD is determined by the number of criteria met, with 2-3 indicating a mild disorder, 4-5 a moderate disorder, and 6 or more a severe disorder (APA, 2013).

While the specific signs and symptoms of SUDs can vary depending on the substance and the individual, there are some common warning signs that can indicate a problem:

1. Tolerance: Needing more of the substance to get the same effect.

2. Withdrawal: Experiencing physical or psychological symptoms when not using the substance, such as nausea, shaking, sweating, or anxiety.

3. Loss of control: Using more of the substance than planned, or for longer than intended.

4. Unsuccessfully trying to quit: Having a persistent desire to cut down or stop using the substance, but being unable to do so.

5. Time consumed: Spending a lot of time obtaining, using, or recovering from the effects of the substance.

6. Neglecting responsibilities: Failing to fulfill obligations at work, school, or home due to substance use.

7. Relationship problems: Continuing to use the substance despite it causing or exacerbating social or interpersonal problems.

8. Giving up activities: Reducing or giving up important social, occupational, or recreational activities because of substance use.

9. Hazardous use: Using the substance in physically dangerous situations, such as while driving or operating machinery.

10. Health problems: Continuing to use the substance despite physical or psychological problems caused or worsened by use.

11. Cravings: Experiencing a strong desire or urge to use the substance.

In adolescents, some additional signs of SUDs may include changes in academic performance, changes in friend groups, secretiveness about activities, changes in appearance or hygiene, and increased conflict with family or authority figures (Winters et al., 2014).

It's important to note that the presence of these signs and symptoms does not necessarily indicate an SUD. Many of these behaviors can be normal parts of adolescent development or can be caused by other factors such as mental health problems, stress, or trauma. However, when these behaviors are causing significant impairment or distress, or when multiple signs are present, it may indicate the need for further assessment and intervention.

The development of an SUD is influenced by a complex interplay of biological, psychological, and social factors. Genetic factors can make some individuals more vulnerable to developing SUDs, particularly if there is a family history of substance use problems (Stone et al., 2012). Mental health problems, such as depression, anxiety, ADHD, and conduct disorder, can also increase the risk of developing an SUD, as youth may use substances to cope with symptoms (Armstrong & Costello, 2002).

Social and environmental factors also play a significant role. Easy availability of substances, social norms that promote or tolerate substance use, and peer influence can all contribute to the development of SUDs (Stone et al., 2012). Family factors, such as parental substance use, poor parenting practices, and family conflict, can also increase risk (Lander et al., 2013).

Prevention and early intervention are crucial for reducing the risk of SUDs in youth. Universal prevention programs, which target all youth regardless of risk, can help promote healthy behaviors and reduce the initiation of substance use (Griffin & Botvin, 2010). Selective prevention programs target youth who are at increased risk due to biological, psychological, or social factors, while indicated prevention programs target youth who are already showing early signs of problematic use (Winters et al., 2007).

For youth who have developed SUDs, treatment is essential. The most effective treatments for adolescent SUDs are comprehensive, addressing not only the substance use but also the psychological, social, and family factors that contribute to it (Hogue et al., 2014). Evidence-based treatments include cognitive-behavioral therapy, which helps youth identify and change problematic thoughts and behaviors; motivational interviewing, which helps increase intrinsic motivation for change; and family-based therapies, which address family dynamics and communication (Winters et al., 2014).

Medications can also play a role in treatment for some SUDs. For example, buprenorphine and methadone are effective for treating opioid use disorder, while naltrexone can be used for alcohol use disorder (Winters et al., 2014). However, medication should always be used in conjunction with psychosocial treatments.

Treatment for SUDs is not a one-size-fits-all approach, and what works for one individual may not work for another. Treatment should be tailored to the specific needs of the individual, taking into account the severity of the disorder, the presence of co-occurring mental health problems, and the individual's readiness for change (Brannigan et al., 2004).

Recovery from an SUD is a long-term process that often involves setbacks and challenges. Relapse, or a return to substance use after a period of abstinence, is common and should be seen as a part of the recovery process rather than a failure (McLellan et al., 2000). Ongoing support, through peer support groups, ongoing therapy, or recovery support services, can help individuals maintain their gains and prevent relapse (McKay, 2009).

In conclusion, substance use disorders in youth are a significant public health problem with wide-ranging consequences for individuals, families, and society. The adolescent brain is particularly vulnerable to the effects of substance use, with the potential for long-term impacts on cognitive, emotional, and social functioning. Understanding the signs and symptoms of SUDs, as well as the factors that contribute to their development, is crucial for effective prevention and intervention.

Comprehensive, evidence-based treatment that addresses the multiple influences on substance use is essential for promoting recovery and preventing the long-term harms of SUDs. But treatment is not enough - we must also address the broader social, cultural, and environmental factors that contribute to substance use problems. This requires a coordinated effort across multiple sectors, including healthcare, education, social services, and policy.

By investing in prevention, early intervention, and treatment, we can reduce the burden of SUDs on youth and families and promote healthy development and well-being for all youth. This is not an easy task, but it is a necessary one if we are to build a healthier, more resilient future for our youth and our society.

Chapter 3. The anxiety-Substance Abuse Connection

How Anxiety and Substance Abuse Fuel Each Other in a Vicious Cycle

Anxiety and substance abuse are two of the most common mental health issues, and they often co-occur, creating a vicious cycle that can be difficult to break. Anxiety disorders, which include generalized anxiety disorder, panic disorder, social anxiety disorder, and specific phobias, affect about 18% of the adult population in the United States (Kessler et al., 2005). Substance use disorders, which involve the problematic use of alcohol, tobacco, or illicit drugs, affect about 10% of the population (SAMHSA, 2020).

The relationship between anxiety and substance abuse is complex and bidirectional. Anxiety can lead to substance abuse as individuals attempt to self-medicate their symptoms, while substance abuse can also cause or worsen anxiety. This creates a feedback loop where each condition reinforces the other, making it harder for individuals to recover from either disorder.

There are several reasons why anxiety and substance abuse often co-occur. First, both conditions share some common risk factors, such as genetics, trauma, and stress (Brady & Sinha, 2005). Individuals who are genetically predisposed to anxiety may also be more vulnerable to developing substance use problems, particularly if they grow up in environments with high levels of stress or trauma.

Second, the symptoms of anxiety can be very distressing and can interfere with daily functioning. Individuals with anxiety may turn to substances as a way to cope with these symptoms. Alcohol and certain drugs, such as benzodiazepines and opioids, can have immediate anxiolytic effects, reducing feelings of anxiety and promoting relaxation (Parrott & Kassel, 1990). However, this relief is temporary and often comes at a cost.

Over time, repeated use of substances to manage anxiety can lead to the development of tolerance and dependence (Kushner et al., 2000). As tolerance develops, individuals need higher and higher doses of the substance to achieve the same effects. This can quickly escalate to problematic use and addiction. Dependence means that the body has adapted to the presence of the substance and goes through withdrawal when the substance is removed.

Substance abuse can also directly contribute to anxiety. Many substances, including alcohol, cocaine, and amphetamines, can cause anxiety symptoms during intoxication or withdrawal (Gunn & Brown, 2022). Alcohol, for example, is a central nervous system depressant that can initially produce feelings of relaxation. However, as the body metabolizes the alcohol, it can lead to a rebound effect, causing symptoms of anxiety and agitation (Randall et al., 1998).

Chronic substance abuse can also lead to changes in brain structure and function that can cause or worsen anxiety. For example, long-term alcohol use can lead to deficits in the brain's serotonin and GABA systems, which are involved in regulating mood and anxiety (Nutt et al., 1999). Chronic cocaine use can cause changes in the brain's stress response system, leading to increased sensitivity to stress and anxiety (Fox et al., 2008).

The cycle of anxiety and substance abuse can be further reinforced by the social and personal consequences of substance use. Substance abuse can lead to problems in relationships, work, and health, which can increase stress and anxiety. The stigma and shame associated with substance use can also contribute to anxiety and make it harder for individuals to seek help.

Breaking the cycle of anxiety and substance abuse requires addressing both disorders simultaneously. Traditional approaches that treat each disorder separately are often ineffective, as untreated anxiety can lead to relapse in substance abuse, and ongoing substance use can interfere with anxiety treatment (Smith & Book, 2010).

Self-Medicating Anxiety with Drugs/Alcohol and the Risk of Addiction

Self-medication is a common phenomenon in individuals with anxiety disorders. Self-medication refers to the use of substances, often without a prescription or in ways not prescribed, to alleviate symptoms of a mental health condition

(Khantzian, 1997). For individuals with anxiety, substances can provide a quick and easy way to reduce feelings of fear, worry, and tension.

Alcohol is one of the most commonly used substances for self-medication of anxiety. Alcohol is a central nervous system depressant that can produce feelings of relaxation and reduce inhibitions. For individuals with social anxiety, alcohol can make it easier to interact with others and reduce fear of negative evaluation (Carrigan & Randall, 2003). For those with generalized anxiety, alcohol can provide a temporary respite from chronic worry and tension.

Benzodiazepines, a class of prescription sedatives, are also frequently used to self-medicate anxiety. Benzodiazepines like Xanax (alprazolam), Valium (diazepam), and Ativan (lorazepam) are fast-acting and can significantly reduce anxiety symptoms (Longo & Johnson, 2000). They work by enhancing the effects of GABA, a neurotransmitter that reduces neural excitability.

While alcohol and benzodiazepines can provide immediate relief from anxiety, their use for self-medication carries significant risks. The most significant risk is the development of addiction. Substance use disorders are characterized by compulsive drug seeking and use despite negative consequences (APA, 2013).

The risk of developing a substance use disorder is particularly high when substances are used to cope with mental health symptoms. This is because the immediate reinforcing effects of the substance (i.e., the reduction in anxiety) can lead to repeated use. Over time, tolerance develops, meaning that higher and higher doses are needed to achieve the same effects (Kushner et al., 2000).

As substance use escalates, individuals can become physically and psychologically dependent. Physical dependence occurs when the body adapts to the presence of the substance and goes through withdrawal when the substance is removed. Psychological dependence occurs when individuals feel they need the substance to function normally or cope with stress (Goodman et al., 2002).

Addiction is a serious condition that can have devastating consequences. Substance use disorders are associated with a wide range of health problems, including liver disease, cardiovascular disease, and neurological damage (McLellan et al., 2000). They can also lead to social, occupational, and legal problems, such as job loss, financial instability, and criminal charges.

Moreover, self-medicating anxiety with substances can actually worsen anxiety in the long run. While substances may provide temporary relief, they do not address the underlying causes of anxiety. In fact, substance use can interfere with the development of healthy coping skills and can prevent individuals from learning to manage their anxiety in adaptive ways (Menary et al., 2011).

Substance use can also cause or worsen anxiety through several mechanisms. Alcohol and many drugs can cause anxiety symptoms during intoxication or withdrawal (Gunn & Brown, 2022). Chronic substance use can also lead to changes in brain function that can increase vulnerability to anxiety (Zhao et al., 2021).

Therefore, while self-medication of anxiety with substances may provide short-term relief, it is not a safe or effective long-term solution. Individuals with anxiety who are self-medicating with substances should seek professional help to develop healthier coping strategies and address their substance use.

Substance-Induced Anxiety Disorders

Substance-induced anxiety disorders are mental health conditions that are directly caused by the effects of a substance. These disorders are distinct from primary anxiety disorders, which develop independently of substance use. Substance-induced anxiety disorders can occur during intoxication with a substance or during withdrawal from a substance (APA, 2013).

Many substances can cause anxiety symptoms. Stimulants like cocaine, amphetamines, and even caffeine can cause feelings of nervousness, restlessness, and panic (Watling et al., 2016). Hallucinogens like LSD and psilocybin can cause intense anxiety and fear, especially in unfamiliar or uncontrolled settings (Johnson et al., 2008). Cannabis, particularly in high doses, can also cause acute anxiety and panic attacks (Sexton et al., 2019).

Alcohol and sedatives like benzodiazepines can cause anxiety symptoms during withdrawal. Alcohol withdrawal syndrome can include severe anxiety, agitation, and even panic attacks (Gunn & Brown, 2022). Benzodiazepine withdrawal can also be severe and can include rebound anxiety that is worse than the initial anxiety the drugs were used to treat (Lader, 2011).

Opioids, while often associated with feelings of euphoria and relaxation, can also cause anxiety. This is particularly true during opioid withdrawal, which can include severe anxiety and agitation (Kosten & George, 2002). Chronic opioid use can also lead to changes in the brain's stress response system, increasing vulnerability to anxiety (Sharma et al., 2019).

Substance-induced anxiety disorders can be challenging to diagnose because they can mimic primary anxiety disorders. The key distinguishing feature is the temporal relationship between substance use and anxiety symptoms. For a diagnosis of a substance-induced anxiety disorder, the anxiety symptoms must have developed during or soon after substance intoxication or withdrawal and must be severeenough to warrant clinical attention (APA, 2013).

Treatment for substance-induced anxiety disorders typically involves a combination of interventions aimed at managing the acute anxiety symptoms and treating the underlying substance use disorder. Benzodiazepines, which are commonly used to treat primary anxiety disorders, are generally avoided in individuals with substance use disorders due to the risk of abuse and dependence (Guina & Merrill, 2018). Instead, antidepressants like selective serotonin reuptake inhibitors

(SSRIs) may be used to manage anxiety symptoms (Ijaz et al., 2018).

Psychosocial interventions are also crucial in the treatment of substance-induced anxiety disorders. Cognitive-behavioral therapy (CBT) can help individuals identify and change maladaptive thoughts and behaviors related to substance use and anxiety (McHugh et al., 2010). Exposure therapy, a type of CBT that involves gradually confronting feared situations, can be particularly helpful for individuals with phobias or panic disorder (Barlow, 2002).

Motivational interviewing, a client-centered approach that aims to increase intrinsic motivation for change, can be effective in helping individuals reduce their substance use (Miller & Rollnick, 2012). Contingency management, which involves providing rewards for abstinence or other treatment-related goals, has also shown promise in treating substance use disorders (Petry, 2006).

In addition to formal treatment, self-help strategies can be useful for managing anxiety and promoting recovery from substance use disorders. These may include relaxation techniques like deep breathing and progressive muscle relaxation, exercise, and mindfulness meditation (Kim et al., 2013). Support groups like Alcoholics Anonymous and Narcotics Anonymous can provide a sense of community and accountability for individuals in recovery (Kelly, 2017).

Preventing substance-induced anxiety disorders involves addressing substance use early and promoting healthy coping strategies. Education about the risks of substance use, including the potential for anxiety and other mental health problems, can help deter individuals from using substances to cope with stress or emotional distress. Promoting access to mental health services and teaching healthy coping skills in schools and community settings can also help prevent the development of substance use disorders and co-occurring anxiety (Stockings et al., 2016).

Challenges in Treating Co-Occurring Anxiety and Substance Use Disorders

Treating co-occurring anxiety and substance use disorders can be challenging for several reasons. First, the symptoms of each disorder can interact and exacerbate each other. Anxiety can drive substance use as individuals attempt to self-medicate, while substance use can worsen anxiety through the direct effects of intoxication and withdrawal, as well as through the lifestyle and health consequences of addiction (Smith & Book, 2010).

Second, individuals with co-occurring disorders often have more severe symptoms and poorer treatment outcomes compared to those with either disorder alone. They may have higher rates of relapse, more severe withdrawal symptoms, and more psychosocial problems (Kushner et al., 2005). They may also have other co-occurring mental health conditions, such as depression or post-traumatic stress disorder, which can further complicate treatment (Grant et al., 2004).

Third, the traditional separation of mental health and substance abuse treatment systems can make it difficult for individuals to receive comprehensive care. Mental health providers may not be equipped to handle substance use issues, while substance abuse treatment providers may not have the expertise to manage anxiety disorders (Murthy & Lakshman, 2021). This can lead to fragmented and ineffective care.

Fourth, pharmacological treatments for anxiety, such as benzodiazepines, can be problematic for individuals with substance use disorders. Benzodiazepines have a high potential for abuse and can be dangerous when combined with other substances, particularly alcohol and opioids (Guina & Merrill, 2018). Antidepressants, while safer, can take several weeks to take effect, which can be challenging for individuals in early recovery (Otto et al., 2005).

Finally, the stigma associated with both mental illness and substance abuse can be a significant barrier to treatment. Individuals may be reluctant to seek help due to shame, fear of judgment, or concerns about negative consequences like job loss or legal problems (Corrigan, 2004). The stigma can also contribute to a lack of understanding and support from family, friends, and the broader community.

Despite these challenges, effective treatment for co-occurring anxiety and substance use disorders is possible. Integrated treatment, which addresses both disorders simultaneously, has been shown to be more effective than separate treatment for each disorder (Kelly et al., 2012). Integrated treatment typically involves a multidisciplinary team of mental health and substance abuse professionals working together to provide comprehensive care.

Cognitive-behavioral therapy (CBT) is one of the most well-studied and effective treatments for both anxiety and substance use disorders. CBT helps individuals identify and change maladaptive thoughts and behaviors related to anxiety and substance use (Combes & Arespacochaga, 2021). It can be delivered in individual, group, or online formats and can be tailored to the specific needs of each individual.

Exposure therapy, a type of CBT, can be particularly helpful for individuals with phobias, panic disorder, or post-traumatic stress disorder. Exposure therapy involves gradually confronting feared situations or memories in a safe and controlled environment (Barlow, 2002). Over time, this can help reduce the intensity and frequency of anxiety symptoms.

Motivational interviewing is another effective approach for treating substance use disorders. Motivational interviewing is a client-centered approach that aims to increase intrinsic motivation for change (Miller & Rollnick, 2012). It involves exploring and resolving ambivalence about change and supporting self-efficacy.

Medications can also play a role in the treatment of co-occurring anxiety and substance use disorders. Antidepressants, particularly selective serotonin reuptake inhibitors (SSRIs), can be effective for managing anxiety symptoms (Ijaz et al., 2018). They are generally considered safer than benzodiazepines for individuals with substance use disorders. However, they can take several weeks to take effect, so they are often used in conjunction with therapy and other support strategies.

For individuals with opioid use disorder, medication-assisted treatment (MAT) can be life-saving. MAT involves the use of medications like methadone, buprenorphine, or naltrexone to reduce cravings and withdrawal symptoms (Volkow et al., 2014). When combined with therapy and support, MAT can significantly improve outcomes for individuals with opioid addiction.

In addition to formal treatment, peer support can be a valuable resource for individuals with co-occurring disorders. Peer support involves receiving support from others who have experienced similar challenges. This can include 12-step groups like Alcoholics Anonymous or Narcotics Anonymous, as well as mental health support groups (Bassuk et al., 2016). Peer support can provide a sense of community, reduce isolation, and offer practical strategies for managing symptoms and maintaining recovery.

Family involvement in treatment can also be beneficial. Addiction and mental illness can have a significant impact on families, causing stress, conflict, and dysfunction (Lander et al., 2013). Family therapy can help improve communication, resolve conflicts, and promote a supportive home environment. It can also educate family members about addiction and mental illness and teach them strategies for supporting their loved one's recovery (Lander et al., 2013).

Lifestyle changes can also support recovery from co-occurring anxiety and substance use disorders. Regular exercise has been shown to reduce anxiety and improve mood (Stubbs et al., 2017). Mindfulness practices like meditation and yoga can help reduce stress and promote relaxation (Hoffmann, 2010). Healthy eating and sleep habits can also improve overall health and well-being.

In conclusion, co-occurring anxiety and substance use disorders are complex conditions that require comprehensive and integrated treatment. While there are significant challenges in providing effective care, there are also many evidence-based strategies that can help individuals achieve and maintain recovery. These include cognitive-behavioral therapy, exposure therapy, motivational interviewing, medication-assisted treatment, peer support, family involvement, and lifestyle changes.

Effective treatment requires a collaborative approach that addresses the unique needs of each individual. It should be culturally sensitive, trauma-informed, and grounded in a respect for the individual's autonomy and right to self-determination. Treatment should also be accessible, affordable, and of sufficient duration to promote long-term recovery.

Preventing the development of co-occurring anxiety and substance use disorders is also crucial. This requires addressing the social determinants of health, such as poverty, trauma, and lack of access to education and healthcare. It also involves promoting mental health literacy, reducing stigma, and increasing access to evidence-based prevention and early intervention programs.

Ultimately, addressing co-occurring anxiety and substance use disorders requires a societal commitment to promoting mental health and well-being for all individuals. This includes investing in research, education, and clinical care, as well as working to create a more just and equitable society. By working together, we can reduce the burden of these conditions and help individuals achieve meaningful and sustained recovery.

Chapter 4. Risk and Protective Factors

Biological, Psychological, and Social Factors that Increase Risk

The development of mental health disorders, including anxiety and substance use disorders, is influenced by a complex interplay of biological, psychological, and social factors. Understanding these risk factors is crucial for developing effective prevention and intervention strategies.

Biological factors that can increase the risk of anxiety and substance use disorders include genetic predisposition, neurochemical imbalances, and structural or functional brain abnormalities. Studies have shown that anxiety disorders and substance use disorders tend to run in families, suggesting a genetic component (Merikangas et al., 1998; Kendler et al., 2003). Specific genetic variations, such as those affecting the serotonin transporter gene or the dopamine receptor gene, have been associated with increased vulnerability to these disorders (Lesch et al., 1996; Noble, 2000).

Neurochemical imbalances, particularly in the brain's serotonin, dopamine, and GABA systems, have also been implicated in the development of anxiety and substance use disorders. Serotonin is involved in regulating mood and anxiety, while dopamine is involved in reward and motivation (Müller & Homberg, 2015). Disruptions in these neurotransmitter systems, whether due to genetic factors, stress, or substance use, can contribute to the development of mental health disorders.

Structural and functional brain abnormalities have also been observed in individuals with anxiety and substance use disorders. For example, individuals with anxiety disorders may have reduced volume in the hippocampus, a brain region involved in memory and emotion regulation (Irle et al., 2010). Individuals with substance use disorders may have reduced volume in the prefrontal cortex, a brain region involved in decision-making and impulse control (Goldstein & Volkow, 2011).

Psychological factors that can increase the risk of anxiety and substance use disorders include personality traits, cognitive styles, and coping mechanisms. Certain personality traits, such as neuroticism (a tendency to experience negative emotions) and impulsivity (a tendency to act without thinking), have been associated with increased risk of these disorders (Lahey, 2009). Cognitive styles characterized by negative self-talk, rumination, and catastrophic thinking can also contribute to the development and maintenance of anxiety (Brozovich & Heimberg, 2008).

Maladaptive coping mechanisms, such as avoidance and substance use, can also increase the risk of anxiety and substance use disorders. Avoidance involves escaping or avoiding situations that trigger anxiety, which can provide short-term relief but can also reinforce the anxiety in the long-term (Barlow, 2002). Substance use can be a way of coping with negative emotions or stressors, but it can also lead to the development of addiction and other health problems (Khantzian, 1997).

Social factors that can increase the risk of anxiety and substance use disorders include family dynamics, peer influences, and societal pressures. Family dynamics characterized by conflict, inconsistency, or lack of warmth and support can contribute to the development of mental health problems (Repetti et al., 2002). Peer influences, particularly during adolescence, can also be powerful risk factors. Associating with peers who engage in substance use or have positive attitudes towards drugs can increase the likelihood of experimentation and problematic use (Simons-Morton & Chen, 2006).

Societal pressures, such as academic or occupational stress, financial strain, and discrimination, can also contribute to the development of anxiety and substance use disorders. Chronic stress can lead to changes in the brain and body that increase vulnerability to mental health problems (McEwen, 2012). Discrimination and marginalization can also have profound effects on mental health, particularly for individuals from minority or disadvantaged groups (Williams et al., 2003).

The Role of Family History, Trauma, and Adverse Childhood Experiences

Family history, trauma, and adverse childhood experiences are significant risk factors for the development of anxiety and substance use disorders. Understanding these factors can help inform prevention and treatment efforts.

Family history is one of the strongest predictors of mental health problems. Children of parents with anxiety disorders or substance use disorders are at increased risk of developing these conditions themselves (Woodward & Fergusson, 2001). This increased risk is likely due to a combination of genetic and environmental factors. Genetically, children may inherit a vulnerability to these disorders. Environmentally, they may be exposed to stressful or chaotic home environments, learn maladaptive coping strategies, or have reduced access to protective factors like supportive relationships and resources (Biederman et al., 2006).

Trauma, whether experienced directly or witnessed, can also have a profound impact on mental health. Traumatic events can include physical or sexual abuse, domestic violence, natural disasters, car accidents, or the sudden loss of a loved one. Trauma can lead to the development of post-traumatic stress disorder (PTSD), which is characterized by intrusive memories, avoidance, negative changes in thinking and mood, and hyperarousal (APA, 2013).

Trauma can also increase the risk of other anxiety disorders and substance use disorders. Individuals who have experienced trauma may use substances as a way to cope with painful memories or emotions (Roberts et al., 2011). They may also have difficulty regulating their emotions, trusting others, or feeling safe in the world, which can contribute to the development of anxiety (Vander Kolk, 2014).

Adverse childhood experiences (ACEs) are a specific type of trauma that occur during childhood. ACEs can include abuse (physical, emotional, or sexual), neglect (physical or emotional), and household dysfunction (such as having a parent with a mental illness or substance use disorder, witnessing domestic violence, or having a parent who is incarcerated) (Felitti et al., 1998).

ACEs are surprisingly common, with over 60% of adults in the United States reporting at least one ACE (Merrick et al., 2019). ACEs can have a cumulative effect on health and well-being, with higher numbers of ACEs associated with increased risk of mental health problems, substance abuse, and physical health conditions like heart disease and cancer (Hughes et al., 2017).

The impact of ACEs is thought to be mediated by toxic stress, which is the prolonged activation of the body's stress response system in the absence of protective relationships (Harvard University, 2021). Toxic stress can lead to changes in brain structure and function, particularly in areas involved in emotion regulation, impulse control, and memory (Shonkoff et al., 2012). These changes can increase vulnerability to mental health problems and maladaptive coping strategies like substance use.

Preventing and mitigating the impact of trauma and ACEs is a critical public health priority. This can involve strategies at the individual, family, and community levels. At the individual level, providing trauma-informed care and teaching coping and resilience skills can help individuals who have experienced trauma (SAMHSA, 2014). At the family level, supporting positive parenting practices and promoting secure attachment can help buffer the impact of stress and adversity (Barth et al., 2005). At the community level, policies and programs that reduce poverty, promote social cohesion, and increase access to mental health services can help prevent and address the consequences of trauma and ACEs (Larkin et al., 2014).

Protective Factors that Build Resilience

While risk factors can increase the likelihood of developing anxiety and substance use disorders, protective factors can help mitigate this risk and promote resilience. Resilience refers to the ability to adapt and cope with adversity, and it is influenced by a variety of individual, family, and community factors (Luthar et al., 2000).

At the individual level, protective factors include personal characteristics and skills that help individuals navigate stress and challenges. These can include:

1. Positive coping skills: The ability to manage stress in healthy ways, such as through exercise, relaxation techniques, or seeking support from others (Compas et al., 2001).

2. Emotion regulation skills: The ability to recognize, understand, and manage one's emotions in adaptive ways (Gross & Muñoz, 1995).

3. Problem-solving skills: The ability to identify problems, generate solutions, and implement strategies to address challenges (Nezu & Nezu, 2001).

4. Self-efficacy: The belief in one's ability to succeed and overcome obstacles (Bandura, 1997).

5. Optimism and hope: The ability to maintain a positive outlook and expect good things in the future (Scheier & Carver, 1992).

At the family level, protective factors include characteristics of the family environment that promote safety, stability, and support. These can include:

1. Supportive parent-child relationships: Relationships characterized by warmth, responsiveness, and appropriate boundaries (Baumrind, 1991).

2. Family cohesion: A sense of emotional bonding and support among family members (Olson et al., 1985).

3. Clear expectations and consistent discipline: Predictable rules and consequences that are communicated and enforced in a fair and consistent manner4. Parental monitoring: The extent to which parents are aware of and involved in their children's activities and relationships (Dishion & McMahon, 1998).

5. Family engagement in school and community: Family participation in and support for their children's educational and extracurricular activities (Henderson & Mapp, 2002).

At the community level, protective factors include characteristics of the neighborhood, school, and broader social environment that promote safety, belonging, and opportunity. These can include:

1. Safe and supportive neighborhoods: Communities with low levels of crime, violence, and poverty, and high levels of social cohesion and collective efficacy (Sampson et al., 1997).

2. Positive school climate: Schools characterized by supportive teacher-student relationships, high expectations for achievement, and opportunities for participation and leadership (Cohen et al., 2009).

3. Extracurricular activities: Opportunities for youth to engage in structured, supervised activities outside of school, such as sports, clubs, or community service (Mahoney et al., 2005).

4. Mentoring relationships: Connections with caring, supportive adults who can provide guidance, advice, and encouragement (Rhodes et al., 2006).

5. Access to mental health and substance abuse services: The availability and accessibility of prevention, treatment, and

recovery support services in the community (Levine & Ligenza, 2019).

Building resilience involves cultivating these protective factors at multiple levels. For individuals, this can involve teaching skills like coping, emotion regulation, and problem-solving through evidence-based programs like cognitive-behavioral therapy (Gillham et al., 2007). For families, this can involve providing support and education to promote positive parenting practices and family relationships (Sanders, 1999). For communities, this can involve implementing policies and programs that promote safety, equity, and access to resources (Mercy & Saul, 2009).

It's important to note that resilience is not a fixed trait, but rather a dynamic process that can be developed and strengthened over time. Resilience is also context-specific, meaning that what helps an individual cope in one situation may not be effective in another (Luthar & Cicchetti, 2000). Therefore, efforts to build resilience should be tailored to the unique needs and circumstances of each individual and community.

The Importance of Early Intervention and Prevention

Given the significant impact of anxiety and substance use disorders on individuals, families, and society, early intervention and prevention are critical. Early intervention refers to identifying and treating mental health problems as soon as possible, while prevention refers to efforts to stop mental health problems from developing in the first place (Tolan & Dodge, 2005).

Early intervention is important because mental health problems can be more effectively treated when they are identified early. For anxiety disorders, early intervention can prevent the development of more severe and chronic forms of the disorder (Hirshfeld-Becker & Biederman, 2002). For substance use disorders, early intervention can prevent the progression from experimentation to problematic use and addiction (Stockings et al., 2016).

Early intervention strategies can include screening for mental health problems in primary care, schools, and other community settings (Eaton et al., 2008). Screening tools like the Generalized Anxiety Disorder 7-item scale (GAD-7) or the Drug Abuse Screening Test (DAST-10) can help identify individuals who may be at risk and in need of further assessment or treatment (Spitzer et al., 2006; Skinner, 1982). Brief interventions, such as motivational interviewing or psychoeducation, can also be effective for individuals with mild to moderate symptoms (Henry-Edwards et al., 2003).

For individuals with more severe symptoms, early intervention may involve referral to specialized mental health or substance abuse treatment services. Treatment options can include therapy (such as cognitive-behavioral therapy or family therapy), medication (such as antidepressants or medication-assisted treatment for opioid addiction), or a combination of both (Hales et al., 2014). The specific treatment approach should be tailored to the individual's needs, preferences, and circumstances.

Prevention is also critical for reducing the burden of anxiety and substance use disorders. Prevention strategies can be universal (aimed at the general population), selective (aimed at groups at higher risk), or indicated (aimed at individuals showing early signs of a disorder) (Institute of Medicine, 2009).

Universal prevention strategies can include school-based programs that teach social and emotional skills, media campaigns that promote mental health literacy and reduce stigma, and policies that restrict access to alcohol and other drugs (Banerjee et al., 2018; Grube & Nygaard, 2001; World Health Organization, 2018). Selective prevention strategies can target groups at higher risk, such as children of parents with mental illness or individuals living in poverty, and provide additional support and resources (Siegenthaler et al., 2012; Yonas et al., 2010). Indicated prevention strategies can involve screening and early intervention for individuals showing early signs of anxiety or substance misuse (Greenberg & Abenavoli, 2017).

Prevention efforts should be informed by research on risk and protective factors and should be developmentally appropriate. For example, programs for young children may focus on promoting secure attachment and teaching emotional regulation skills, while programs for adolescents may focus on resisting peer pressure and developing healthy coping strategies (Webster-Stratton, 2001; Botvin & Griffin, 2014).

Effective prevention also requires a coordinated, multi-sector approach that involves families, schools, healthcare providers, community organizations, and policymakers. The Icelandic

Model of Adolescent Substance Use Prevention is a notable example of a successful, community-based prevention approach. This model involved increasing parental monitoring, promoting participation in organized activities, and restricting access to substances, and resulted in significant reductions in adolescent substance use (Sigfúsdóttir et al., 2009).

Despite the clear benefits of early intervention and prevention, there are several barriers to implementing these strategies. These can include limited access to mental health services, particularly in underserved communities; stigma and cultural beliefs that discourage help-seeking; and funding and policy priorities that focus on treatment rather than prevention (Corrigan, 2004; Garland et al., 2013).

Overcoming these barriers will require a concerted effort to prioritize mental health, increase funding for prevention and early intervention services, and integrate mental health into primary care and other community settings. It will also require addressing the social determinants of health, such as poverty, discrimination, and lack of education, which can contribute to the development of mental health problems (World Health Organization, 2014).

In conclusion, early intervention and prevention are essential for reducing the burden of anxiety and substance use disorders. By identifying and treating mental health problems early, and by implementing evidence-based prevention strategies at the individual, family, and community levels, we can promote resilience and well-being for all. This will require a collaborative, multi-sector approach that addresses the biological, psychological, and social factors that influence mental health. With commitment and investment, we can create a future where all individuals have the opportunity to thrive and reach their full potential.

Chapter 5: Healthy Coping Strategies for Anxiety

Evidence-Based Treatments for Anxiety

Anxiety disorders are among the most common mental health conditions, affecting millions of people worldwide. Fortunately, there are several evidence-based treatments that can effectively reduce anxiety symptoms and improve quality of life.

Cognitive-behavioral therapy (CBT) is one of the most well-established treatments for anxiety disorders. CBT is based on the idea that thoughts, feelings, and behaviors are interconnected, and that changing one can lead to changes in the others (Beck & Clark, 1997). CBT for anxiety typically involves several components:

1. Psychoeducation: Learning about anxiety, its causes, and its effects on the body and mind (Whitfield & Williams, 2004).

2. Cognitive restructuring: Identifying and challenging anxiety-provoking thoughts and beliefs, and replacing them with more balanced and realistic ones (Clark & Beck, 2010).

3. Exposure: Gradually confronting feared situations or objects in a safe and controlled way, in order to reduce avoidance and build confidence (Norton & Price, 2007).

4. Relaxation techniques: Learning and practicing strategies to reduce physical tension and promote a sense of calm, such as deep breathing, progressive muscle relaxation, or guided imagery (Davis et al., 2008).

CBT can be delivered in individual, group, or online formats, and is typically provided by a licensed mental health professional. Numerous studies have demonstrated the effectiveness of CBT for various anxiety disorders, including generalized anxiety disorder, panic disorder, social anxiety disorder, and specific phobias (Carpenter et al., 2018; Hoffmann et al., 2012).

Medications can also be an effective treatment option for anxiety disorders. The most commonly prescribed medications for anxiety are antidepressants, particularly selective serotonin reuptake inhibitors (SSRIs) and serotonin-norepinephrine reuptake inhibitors (SNRIs) (Bandelow et al., 2017). These medications work by increasing the levels of neurotransmitters like serotonin and norepinephrine in the brain, which can help regulate mood and reduce anxiety (Hiemke & Härtter, 2000).

Benzodiazepines, such as alprazolam (Xanax) or lorazepam (Ativan), are another class of medications that can be used to treat anxiety. These medications work by enhancing the effects of GABA, a neurotransmitter that reduces brain activity and promotes relaxation (Nemeroff, 2003). However, benzodiazepines can be habit-forming and may cause side effects like drowsiness or dizziness, so they are typically prescribed only for short-term use (Baldwin et al., 2013).

The choice of medication depends on several factors, including the type and severity of anxiety, the presence of co-occurring conditions, and individual preferences and medical history. Medications are often used in combination with therapy, and regular monitoring by a healthcare provider is important to assess effectiveness and adjust dosage as needed.

In addition to CBT and medications, there are several other evidence-based treatments for anxiety disorders. These include:

1. Acceptance and Commitment Therapy (ACT): A form of therapy that focuses on accepting anxious thoughts and feelings, while committing to valued actions and goals (Forman et al., 2007).

2. Mindfulness-Based Stress Reduction (MBSR): A program that teaches mindfulness skills to help individuals cope with stress and anxiety (Goldin & Gross, 2010).

3. Eye Movement Desensitization and Reprocessing (EMDR): A therapy that uses eye movements or other bilateral stimulation to help process traumatic memories and reduce anxiety (Shapiro & Forrest, 2016).

4. Family and Couples Therapy: Therapy that involves family members or partners to improve communication, problem-solving, and support (Byrne et al., 2004).

The choice of treatment depends on individual needs and preferences, as well as the availability of trained providers. In some cases, a combination of treatments may be most effective.

Lifestyle Changes to Reduce Anxiety

In addition to formal treatment, making lifestyle changes can also help reduce anxiety symptoms and promote overall well-being. These changes can be implemented alongside therapy or medication, or as stand-alone strategies for individuals with mild to moderate anxiety.

Exercise is one of the most effective lifestyle changes for reducing anxiety. Regular physical activity has been shown to reduce symptoms of anxiety and depression, as well as improve sleep, self-esteem, and cognitive function (Craft & Perna, 2004). Exercise may reduce anxiety through several mechanisms, including releasing endorphins (natural pain relievers and mood elevators), reducing muscle tension, and promoting a sense of accomplishment and self-efficacy (Schuch et al., 2016).

The type and amount of exercise that is most effective for reducing anxiety may vary depending on individual preferences and fitness levels. However, guidelines generally recommend at least 150 minutes of moderate-intensity aerobic exercise (such as brisk walking or cycling) or 75 minutes of vigorous-intensity aerobic exercise (such as running or swimming) per week, along with strength training exercises at least twice a week (Physical Activity Guidelines Advisory Committee, 2018).

Sleep hygiene is another important lifestyle factor for reducing anxiety. Sleep disturbances, such as insomnia or excessive sleepiness, are common among individuals with anxiety disorders (Cox & Olatunji, 2016). Poor sleep can exacerbate anxiety symptoms, while getting enough quality sleep can help reduce anxiety and improve overall functioning (Freeman et al., 2017).

To improve sleep hygiene, experts recommend establishing a consistent sleep schedule, creating a relaxing bedtime routine, avoiding caffeine and alcohol close to bedtime, and creating a comfortable sleep environment (Irish et al., 2015). If sleep problems persist, cognitive-behavioral therapy for insomnia (CBT-I) may be an effective treatment option (Van Straten et al., 2018).

Nutrition is another lifestyle factor that can influence anxiety. While research on the relationship between diet and anxiety is still emerging, some studies suggest that certain dietary patterns may be associated with lower rates of anxiety. For example, the Mediterranean diet, which is high in fruits, vegetables, whole grains, and healthy fats, has been linked to lower rates of depression and anxiety (Jacka et al., 2017). Conversely, diets high in processed foods, sugar, and saturated fats have been associated with higher rates of anxiety and other mental health problems (Firth et al., 2019).

Specific nutrients, such as omega-3 fatty acids, probiotics, and B vitamins, may also play a role in reducing anxiety (Rao et al., 2008). However, more research is needed to confirm these effects and determine optimal dosages and sources. In general, a balanced diet that includes a variety of nutrient-dense foods is recommended for overall health and well-being.

Stress management is another key lifestyle strategy for reducing anxiety. Chronic stress can contribute to the development and maintenance of anxiety disorders, as well as other health problems (Thoits, 2010). Effective stress management involves identifying sources of stress, developing coping strategies, and building resilience.

Mindfulness and relaxation techniques, such as deep breathing, progressive muscle relaxation, and meditation, can be helpful for managing stress and reducing anxiety (Khoury et al., 2013). These techniques can help individuals focus on the present moment, reduce muscle tension, and promote a sense of calm and well-being.

Time management and organizational skills can also help reduce stress and anxiety. Creating a schedule, prioritizing tasks, and breaking large projects into smaller, manageable steps can help individuals feel more in control and less overwhelmed (Misra & McKean, 2000).

Social support is another important factor in managing stress and reducing anxiety. Having a strong network of family, friends, or other supportive individuals can provide a sense of belonging, validation, and practical assistance (Cohen & Wills, 1985). Engaging in enjoyable activities and hobbies, whether alone or with others, can also help reduce stress and promote positive emotions (Newman et al., 2014).

It's important to note that making lifestyle changes can be challenging, especially for individuals with severe anxiety or co-occurring conditions. Working with a therapist or other healthcare provider can help individuals identify realistic goals, develop a plan for change, and address any barriers or setbacks that may arise.

Building Distress Tolerance and Emotion Regulation Skills

Distress tolerance and emotion regulation are two important skills for managing anxiety and other difficult emotions. Distress tolerance refers to the ability to withstand and cope with uncomfortable or painful emotions, while emotion regulation refers to the ability to influence which emotions one experiences, when one experiences them, and how one expresses them (Linehan, 2014).

Individuals with anxiety disorders often have difficulty tolerating distress and regulating emotions. They may engage in avoidance behaviors, such as procrastination or substance use, to escape or numb uncomfortable feelings (Hayes et al., 1996). They may also have intense emotional reactions that feel overwhelming and difficult to control (Mennin et al., 2005). Building distress tolerance and emotion regulation skills is an important part of treatment for anxiety disorders. These skills can help individuals cope with anxiety in the moment, as well as reduce the frequency and intensity of anxiety over time.

Dialectical Behavior Therapy (DBT) is one treatment approach that specifically focuses on building distress tolerance and emotion regulation skills. DBT was originally developed for individuals with borderline personality disorder, but has been adapted for use with other conditions, including anxiety disorders (Linehan, 2014).

DBT teaches four main sets of skills:

1. Mindfulness: Learning to focus on the present moment, without judgment (Baer et al., 2008).

2. Distress Tolerance: Learning to cope with crisis situations and tolerate uncomfortable emotions without making them worse (Linehan, 2014).

3. Emotion Regulation: Learning to understand, name, and modify emotions (Linehan, 2014).

4. Interpersonal Effectiveness: Learning to communicate effectively and assert one's needs in relationships (Linehan, 2014).

Specific distress tolerance skills taught in DBT include:

1. Distraction: Engaging in activities that take one's mind off the distressing situation or emotion, such as watching a movie, calling a friend, or doing a puzzle (Linehan, 2014).

2. Self-soothing: Using the five senses to comfort oneself, such as listening to calming music, taking a warm bath, or smelling a favorite scent (Linehan, 2014).

3. Improving the moment: Finding ways to make the current situation more tolerable, such as by finding meaning, creating a relaxing atmosphere, or using positive self-talk (Linehan, 2014).

4. Pros and cons: Weighing the short-term and long-term consequences of different coping options, in order to make a wise decision (Linehan, 2014).

Specific emotion regulation skills taught in DBT include:

1. Identifying and labeling emotions: Learning to recognize and name different emotions, as well as their triggers and effects on the body and mind (Linehan, 2014).

2. Checking the facts: Evaluating whether one's emotional response fits the facts of the situation, and considering alternative interpretations (Linehan, 2014).

3. Opposite action: Acting opposite to one's current emotion, in order to change the emotion (e.g., approaching a feared situation instead of avoiding it) (Linehan, 2014).

4. Problem-solving: Identifying the problem that is causing the emotion, brainstorming solutions, and taking action to solve the problem (Linehan, 2014).

These skills are typically taught in a group format, with opportunities for practice and feedback. Individuals are also encouraged to practice the skills in their daily lives, and to track their progress using diary cards or other tools.

In addition to DBT, there are several other approaches to building distress tolerance and emotion regulation skills. These include:

1. Cognitive-Behavioral Therapy (CBT): CBT teaches skills for identifying and challenging anxiety-provoking thoughts, as well as relaxation and exposure techniques (Norton & Price, 2007).

2. Mindfulness-Based Stress Reduction (MBSR): MBSR teaches mindfulness skills, such as meditation and body awareness, to help individuals cope with stress and anxiety (Kabat-Zinn, 2006).

3. Acceptance and Commitment Therapy (ACT): ACT teaches skills for accepting difficult thoughts and feelings, while committing to valued actions (Hayes et al., 2006).

4. Self-compassion: Self-compassion involves treating oneself with kindness, recognizing one's common humanity, and being mindful of one's emotions (Neff, 2003). Self-compassion has been linked to lower levels of anxiety and greater emotional resilience (MacBeth & Gumley, 2012).

Building distress tolerance and emotion regulation skills takes time and practice. It's important for individuals to be patient with themselves and to seek support from a therapist or other mental health professional when needed.

Accessing Treatment and Support Services

Despite the availability of effective treatments for anxiety disorders, many individuals do not receive the care they need. Barriers to treatment can include lack of awareness, stigma, financial constraints, and limited access to trained providers (Gulliver et al., 2010).

To improve access to treatment and support services, it's important for individuals to be proactive in seeking help. This may involve talking to a primary care provider, contacting a mental health professional, or reaching out to a support group or helpline.

Primary care providers, such as family doctors or nurse practitioners, can be a good first point of contact for individuals with anxiety concerns. They can provide an initial assessment, offer referrals to mental health specialists, and prescribe medications if needed (Patel et al., 2008).

Mental health professionals, such as psychologists, social workers, or licensed counselors, can provide more specialized assessment and treatment services. They may work in private practice, community clinics, hospitals, or other settings. When seeking a mental health professional, it's important to consider factors such as their training, experience, and treatment approach, as well as practical considerations like location, availability, and insurance coverage (American Psychological Association, 2020).

Support groups can be another valuable resource for individuals with anxiety disorders. Support groups provide a safe and confidential space to share experiences, learn coping strategies, and connect with others who understand what it's like to live with anxiety. Support groups may be led by trained facilitators or by peers, and can be held in person or online (Norton et al., 2018).

Helplines and crisis lines can provide immediate support and resources for individuals in distress. These services are typically free, confidential, and available 24/7. Some examples include the National Suicide Prevention Lifeline (1-800-273-TALK), the SAMHSA National Helpline (1-800-662-HELP), and the Crisis Text Line (text HOME to 741741) (NIMH, 2021).

Self-help resources, such as books, websites, and mobile apps, can also be useful for individuals who prefer a more independent approach to managing their anxiety. Self-help resources can provide psychoeducation, coping strategies, and exercises for reducing anxiety symptoms (Andersson et al., 2014). However, it's important to choose reputable and evidence-based resources, and to seek professional help if symptoms are severe or not improving.

For individuals who face barriers to traditional treatment options, telehealth services may be a viable alternative. Telehealth involves providing mental health services remotely, using video conferencing, phone calls, or messaging platforms. Research has shown that telehealth can be effective for treating anxiety disorders, particularly when combined with evidence-based therapies like CBT (Andrews et al., 2018).

Workplace accommodations and school accommodations can also help individuals with anxiety disorders access treatment and support services. These may include flexible scheduling, reduced workload, or permission to take breaks or attend appointments during work or school hours (Job Accommodation Network, 2021).

Ultimately, accessing treatment and support services for anxiety disorders requires a combination of individual effort, social support, and systemic change. Increasing public awareness, reducing stigma, and expanding access to affordable and evidence-based care are all important steps in ensuring that everyone who needs help can get it.

Chapter 6: Substance Abuse Prevention and Treatment

Screening and Early Intervention Programs

Screening and early intervention are critical components of effective substance abuse prevention and treatment. Screening involves assessing individuals for risk factors and early signs of substance abuse, while early intervention involves providing targeted support and resources to prevent the progression to more severe substance use disorders (Sharma & Branscum, 2013).

Screening can be conducted in a variety of settings, including primary care, schools, workplaces, and the criminal justice system (Levy et al., 2016). Screening tools may include questionnaires, structured interviews, or biological tests, such as urine drug screens (Tiet et al., 2008). Some commonly used screening tools for substance abuse include the Alcohol Use Disorders Identification Test (AUDIT), the Drug Abuse Screening Test (DAST), and the CAGE questionnaire (Babor et al., 2001; Skinner, 1982; Ewing, 1984).

The goal of screening is to identify individuals who may be at risk for substance abuse and to provide them with appropriate interventions or referrals. Screening should be conducted in a non-judgmental and confidential manner, with an emphasis on building rapport and trust (Miller et al., 2011).

Early intervention programs can take many forms, depending on the setting, population, and substance of concern. Some common early intervention strategies include:

1. Brief interventions: Short, targeted conversations that aim to increase awareness of substance use and its consequences, and to motivate individuals to change their behavior (Babor & Higgins-Biddle, 2000). Brief interventions can be delivered in person, by phone, or online, and may involve feedback, goal-setting, and referral to additional resources (Tanner-Smith et al., 2015).

2. Motivational interviewing: A client-centered, directive counseling approach that aims to enhance intrinsic motivation for change (Miller & Rollnick, 2012). Motivational interviewing involves exploring and resolving ambivalence, supporting self-efficacy, and developing a plan for change (Miller & Rose, 2009).

3. Psychoeducation: Providing information about substance abuse, its effects on health and well-being, and strategies for reducing harm or quitting (Mintz et al., 1985). Psychoeducation can be delivered individually or in groups, and may involve lectures, discussions, or written materials (Walitzer et al., 2009).

4. Skills training: Teaching specific skills for managing stress, coping with cravings, and resisting peer pressure to use substances (Monti et al., 2001). Skills training may include role-playing, homework assignments, and practice in real-world situations (Larimer et al., 2009).

5. Family interventions: Involving family members in the prevention or early intervention process, with a focus on improving communication, setting boundaries, and supporting positive change (Kumpfer et al., 2003). Family interventions may include family therapy, parent training, or family education programs (Liddle, 2004).

Early intervention programs have been shown to be effective in reducing substance abuse and related problems, particularly among youth and young adults (Tanner-Smith & Lipsey, 2015). For example, the Project ALERT program, a school-based drug prevention curriculum, has been found to reduce the initiation of smoking and drinking among middle school students (Ellickson et al., 2003). The Brief Alcohol Screening and Intervention for College Students (BASICS) program has been shown to reduce drinking and alcohol-related problems among college students (Dimeff et al., 1999).

Despite the potential benefits of screening and early intervention, there are also challenges and barriers to implementation. These may include limited resources, lack of trained personnel, stigma and discrimination, and resistance from individuals or communities (Shah et al., 2013). Overcoming these barriers may require system-level changes, such as integrating substance abuse screening into routine healthcare, providing education and training for healthcare providers, and addressing social determinants of health (Akin et al., 2019).

Motivation Enhancement and Harm Reduction Approaches

Motivation enhancement and harm reduction are two important approaches to substance abuse treatment that focus on meeting individuals where they are at and supporting them in making positive changes.

Motivation enhancement therapy (MET) is a brief, client-centered approach that aims to increase intrinsic motivation for change (Miller et al., 1992). MET is based on the principles of motivational interviewing, which involve expressing empathy, developing discrepancy, rolling with resistance, and supporting self-efficacy (Miller & Rollnick, 2012).

In MET, the therapist works collaboratively with the client to explore their ambivalence about substance use, to identify their goals and values, and to develop a plan for change (Miller et al., 1999). The therapist uses reflective listening, open-ended questions, and affirmations to elicit the client's own reasons for change and to build their confidence in their ability to change (Miller & Rose, 2009).

MET has been shown to be effective in reducing substance abuse and related problems, particularly when combined with other evidence-based treatments (Project MATCH Research Group, 1997). For example, a meta-analysis of 32 randomized controlled trials found that MET had significant effects on reducing alcohol consumption, cannabis use, and other drug use, with effect sizes ranging from small to medium (Lundahl et al., 2010).

Harm reduction is another approach to substance abuse treatment that focuses on reducing the negative consequences of substance use, rather than requiring abstinence (Marlatt & Witkiewitz, 2010). Harm reduction strategies may include providing safe injection equipment, overdose prevention education, or substitution therapies like methadone or buprenorphine (Des Jarlais & Semaan, 2008).

The goal of harm reduction is to meet individuals where they are at and to support them in making positive changes, even if they are not ready or able to quit using substances (Lenton & Single, 1998). Harm reduction approaches recognize that substance use exists on a continuum, and that different individuals may have different goals and needs (Tatarsky & Marlatt, 2010).

Harm reduction has been shown to be effective in reducing the negative consequences of substance use, such as HIV transmission, overdose deaths, and criminal activity (Des Jarlais et al., 2000). For example, needle and syringe exchange programs have been found to reduce HIV transmission among people who inject drugs, without increasing drug use or crime (Aspinall et al., 2014). Medication-assisted treatment with methadone or buprenorphine has been shown to reduce opioid use, overdose deaths, and criminal activity (Mattick et al., 2009).

Despite the evidence supporting motivation enhancement and harm reduction approaches, there are also challenges and criticisms. Some argue that these approaches enable or condone substance use, rather than promoting abstinence

(Kleinig, 2008). Others point out that harm reduction services may be limited or unavailable in some areas, particularly in rural or underserved communities (Des Jarlais et al., 2009).

Overcoming these challenges may require a shift in public attitudes and policies towards substance use, as well as increased funding and support for evidence-based treatment and harm reduction services (Drucker et al., 2016). It may also require collaboration and coordination among healthcare providers, social services, law enforcement, and community organizations (Kuehn, 2013).

Effective Treatments (Behavioral Therapies, Medications, etc.)

There are several effective treatments for substance abuse, including behavioral therapies, medications, and a combination of both. The choice of treatment depends on the specific substance of concern, the severity of the substance use disorder, and individual factors such as co-occurring mental health conditions, social support, and motivation for change (Carroll & Onken, 2005).

Behavioral therapies are a cornerstone of substance abuse treatment, and have been shown to be effective in reducing substance use and related problems (Dutra et al., 2008). Some common behavioral therapies include:

1. Cognitive-behavioral therapy (CBT): CBT focuses on identifying and changing negative thoughts and behaviors that contribute to substance use (McHugh et al., 2010). CBT techniques may include identifying triggers, developing coping skills, and challenging cognitive distortions (Beck, 2011). CBT has been shown to be effective for a range of substance use disorders, including alcohol, cocaine, and opioids (Magill & Ray, 2009).

2. Contingency management (CM): CM involves providing rewards or incentives for achieving specific behavioral goals, such as abstinence or treatment attendance (Petry et al., 2000). CM has been shown to be effective in reducing substance use and increasing treatment retention, particularly for stimulant use disorders (Prendergast et al., 2006).

3. Motivational enhancement therapy (MET): As described earlier, MET is a brief, client-centered approach that aims to increase intrinsic motivation for change (Miller et al., 1992). MET has been shown to be effective inreducing substance use and related problems, particularly when combined with other evidence-based treatments (Project MATCH Research Group, 1997).

4. Family therapy: Family therapy involves working with the individual and their family members to improve communication, set boundaries, and support positive change (Rowe, 2012). Family therapy has been shown to be effective for adolescent substance use disorders, as well as for adults with co-occurring mental health conditions (Baldwin et al., 2012).

Medications can also play an important role in substance abuse treatment, particularly for opioid, alcohol, and tobacco use disorders (Volkow et al., 2014). Some common medications used in substance abuse treatment include:

1. Methadone and buprenorphine: These medications are opioid agonists that can help reduce opioid cravings and withdrawal symptoms, and prevent overdose (Mattick et al., 2009). Methadone and buprenorphine have been shown to be effective in reducing opioid use, HIV risk behaviors, and criminal activity (Connery, 2015).

2. Naltrexone: Naltrexone is an opioid antagonist that can help prevent relapse by blocking the effects of opioids (Minozzi et al., 2011). Naltrexone has been shown to be effective in reducing opioid use and increasing treatment retention, particularly when combined with behavioral therapies (Krupitsky et al., 2011).

3. Disulfiram, acamprosate, and naltrexone: These medications can help reduce alcohol cravings and prevent relapse (Jonas et al., 2014). Disulfiram works by causing an unpleasant reaction when alcohol is consumed, while acamprosate and naltrexone work by modulating neurotransmitter systems involved in alcohol dependence (Zindel & Kranzler, 2014).

4. Varenicline and bupropion: These medications can help reduce tobacco cravings and withdrawal symptoms, and increase the likelihood of quitting smoking (Cahill et al., 2013).

Varenicline works by partially activating nicotinic acetylcholine receptors, while bupropion works by inhibiting the reuptake of dopamine and norepinephrine (Aubin et al., 2014).

Combining behavioral therapies and medications can be particularly effective for substance abuse treatment, as they address different aspects of addiction (Carroll et al., 2014). For example, combining buprenorphine with cognitive-behavioral therapy has been shown to be more effective than either treatment alone for opioid use disorder (Fiellin et al., 2006).

Despite the availability of effective treatments, there are also challenges and barriers to accessing care. These may include limited insurance coverage, lack of trained providers, stigma and discrimination, and logistical barriers such as transportation or childcare (Priester et al., 2016). Addressing these barriers may require policy changes, such as expanding insurance coverage for substance abuse treatment, increasing funding for treatment programs, and integrating substance abuse treatment into primary care settings (Padwa et al., 2015).

Mutual Support Groups and 12-Step Programs

Mutual support groups and 12-step programs are non-professional, peer-led organizations that provide support, guidance, and a sense of community for individuals in recovery from substance abuse (Humphreys et al., 2004). The most well-known 12-step programs are Alcoholics Anonymous (AA) and Narcotics Anonymous (NA), but there are also programs for other substances, such as Cocaine Anonymous (CA) and Marijuana Anonymous (MA) (Kelly et al., 2009).

The 12 steps of AA and other programs involve admitting powerlessness over the substance, surrendering to a higher power, making amends for past wrongs, and continuing to grow spiritually (Alcoholics Anonymous, 2001). Members are encouraged to attend meetings regularly, get a sponsor (a more experienced member who provides guidance and support), and work through the 12 steps with their sponsor (Zemore et al., 2004).

Mutual support groups and 12-step programs have several benefits for individuals in recovery. They provide a sense of belonging and identification with others who have similar experiences, which can reduce feelings of isolation and shame (Tonigan & Rice, 2010). They also provide a structured framework for working on personal growth and development, and for maintaining motivation for change (Kelly et al., 2009).

Research has shown that participating in mutual support groups and 12-step programs can be effective in reducing substance use and related problems, particularly when combined with professional treatment (Kaskutas, 2009). For example, a meta-analysis of 10 studies found that attending AA meetings was associated with improved alcohol outcomes, with a dose-response relationship (meaning that more frequent attendance was associated with better outcomes) (Kelly et al., 2020).

However, there are also some criticisms and limitations of mutual support groups and 12-step programs. Some argue that the emphasis on powerlessness and surrender to a higher power may not be appropriate or effective for all individuals, particularly those with co-occurring mental health conditions or a history of trauma (Peele et al., 2000). Others point out that the 12-step approach may not be compatible with certain cultural or religious beliefs (Connors & Dermen, 1996).

Another limitation of mutual support groups and 12-step programs is that they may not be accessible or available to all individuals, particularly those in rural or underserved areas (Donovan et al., 2013). Additionally, some individuals may not feel comfortable or welcome in traditional 12-step meetings, such as those who identify as LGBTQ+ or those with co-occurring mental health conditions (Melemis, 2015).

To address these limitations, some alternative mutual support groups have emerged, such as SMART Recovery (Self-Management and Recovery Training), which uses a cognitive-behavioral approach and does not rely on the concept of a higher power (Beck et al., 2017). There are also culturally-specific mutual support groups, such as Red Road to Wellbriety for Native American individuals (White Bison, 2002).

Long-Term Recovery Management

Long-term recovery management is an approach to substance abuse treatment that recognizes that recovery is a ongoing process that requires ongoing support and management (Dennis

& Scott, 2007). Rather than focusing solely on achieving abstinence or completing a specific treatment program, long-term recovery management involves providing a continuity of care and support over an extended period of time (Laudet & Humphreys, 2013).

The goal of long-term recovery management is to help individuals maintain their recovery and prevent relapse, while also addressing other areas of their life that may have been affected by their substance use, such as relationships, employment, and physical and mental health (White & Kelly, 2011). This may involve a combination of professional treatment, mutual support groups, and other recovery support services, such as housing, transportation, and vocational training (Laudet et al., 2006).

One key component of long-term recovery management is ongoing monitoring and feedback, which involves regularly assessing an individual's progress and adjusting the plan of care as needed (Scott et al., 2005). This may involve using standardized assessments, such as the Addiction Severity Index or the Recovery Capital Scale, to track changes in substance use, mental health, and other domains over time (McLellan et al., 1992; Groshkova et al., 2013).

Another important aspect of long-term recovery management is peer support, which involves connecting individuals in recovery with others who have similar experiences and can provide guidance, encouragement, and accountability (Valentine et al., 2007). Peer support can take many forms, such as peer mentoring, peer-led support groups, or peer recovery coaching (White, 2009).

Research has shown that long-term recovery management can be effective in improving outcomes for individuals with substance use disorders. For example, a study of individuals with severe opioid use disorder found that those who received ongoing recovery management services, such as medication-assisted treatment and peer support, had significantly better outcomes than those who received standard care (Hser et al., 2016). Another study found that individuals who participated in a recovery management program for alcohol use disorder had significantly higher rates of abstinence and remission than those who received standard care (Dennis et al., 2014).

However, there are also challenges and barriers to implementing long-term recovery management. One challenge is the fragmentation of the current treatment system, which often lacks coordination and continuity of care across different levels of care and service providers (Padwa & Kaplan, 2018). Another challenge is the lack of funding and reimbursement for recovery support services, which can limit their availability and accessibility (Scott et al., 2014).

To address these challenges, some experts have called for a shift towards a recovery-oriented system of care (ROSC), which is a coordinated network of services and supports that is person-centered, strengths-based, and culturally responsive (Sheedy & Whitter, 2009). A ROSC involves collaboration and communication across different service providers, as well asthe involvement of individuals in recovery and their families in the planning and delivery of services (Kaplan, 2008).

Another approach to long-term recovery management is the use of recovery community organizations (RCOs), which are independent, non-profit organizations that provide peer-led recovery support services and advocacy (Valentine et al., 2007). RCOs can serve as a bridge between professional treatment and mutual support groups, and can provide a range of services, such as recovery coaching, education and training, and social and recreational activities (Kaplan et al., 2010).

Despite the challenges and barriers, long-term recovery management is an important approach to substance abuse treatment that recognizes the chronic and relapsing nature of addiction and the need for ongoing support and management. By providing a continuum of care and support, long-term recovery management can help individuals achieve and maintain recovery, while also improving their overall health and well-being.

Chapter 7: Supporting Anxious Youth and Preventing Substance Abuse

How Parents, Schools, Healthcare Providers, and Communities Can Help

Parents, schools, healthcare providers, and communities all play a crucial role in promoting mental health and preventing substance abuse among children and adolescents. By working together and taking a comprehensive approach, these stakeholders can create a supportive environment that fosters resilience, encourages help-seeking behavior, and reduces the risk of mental health problems and substance abuse.

Parents are often the first line of defense in promoting mental health and preventing substance abuse. They can help by creating a warm, nurturing home environment that promotes open communication and emotional well-being (Shonkoff & Garner, 2012). This may involve setting clear expectations and boundaries, providing consistent discipline and supervision, and modeling healthy coping skills and behaviors (Lippold et al., 2014).

Parents can also help by being actively involved in their children's lives, including monitoring their activities and friendships, and staying informed about the signs and symptoms of mental health problems and substance abuse (King et al., 2008). If they notice any concerning changes in their child's behavior or mood, they should seek help from a healthcare provider or mental health professional (Corcoran et al., 2016).

Schools also play a critical role in promoting mental health and preventing substance abuse. They can help by creating a positive school climate that promotes social and emotional learning, academic achievement, and a sense of belonging (Durlak et al., 2011). This may involve implementing evidence-based prevention programs, such as social-emotional learning curricula or school-based mental health services (Greenberg et al., 2017).

Schools can also help by providing training and support for teachers and staff to recognize the signs and symptoms of mental health problems and substance abuse, and to respond appropriately (Reinke et al., 2011). This may involve establishing clear policies and procedures for reporting and responding to concerns, as well as partnering with community-based organizations and healthcare providers to provide additional support and resources (Weist et al., 2014).

Healthcare providers, including pediatricians, mental health professionals, and substance abuse treatment providers, also play a key role in promoting mental health and preventing substance abuse. They can help by providing routine screening and assessment for mental health problems and substance abuse, and by offering evidence-based interventions and treatments (Hagan et al., 2017).

Healthcare providers can also help by collaborating with parents, schools, and other community stakeholders to provide coordinated and comprehensive care (Asarnow et al., 2015). This may involve establishing referral networks and partnerships, sharing information and resources, and working together to develop and implement individualized treatment plans (Kolko & Perrin, 2014).

Communities can also play a vital role in promoting mental health and preventing substance abuse. They can help by creating a supportive and inclusive environment that promotes social connectedness, community engagement, and access to resources and services (Kawachi & Berkman, 2001). This may involve organizing community events and activities, such as youth programs, volunteer opportunities, or cultural celebrations (Sampson et al., 1997).

Communities can also help by advocating for policies and programs that promote mental health and prevent substance abuse, such as increasing funding for mental health and substance abuse services, improving access to healthcare and social services, and promoting public education and awareness (Shim & Compton, 2018).

Combating Stigma and Promoting Mental Health Awareness

Stigma and lack of awareness are significant barriers to seeking help for mental health and substance abuse problems. Stigma refers to the negative attitudes, beliefs, and stereotypes that society holds about individuals with mental illness or substance abuse disorders (Corrigan & Watson, 2002). These attitudes can lead to discrimination, social exclusion, and a reluctance to seek help (Clement et al., 2015).

To combat stigma and promote mental health awareness, it is important to educate the public about the prevalence, causes, and treatment of mental health and substance abuse problems. This may involve providing accurate and evidence-based information through various channels, such as media campaigns, educational programs, or community events (Jorm, 2012).

It is also important to challenge and correct misconceptions and stereotypes about mental illness and substance abuse, and to promote a more compassionate and understanding approach. This may involve sharing personal stories and experiences, highlighting the diversity of individuals affected by mental health and substance abuse problems, and emphasizing the importance of seeking help and support (Corrigan et al., 2012).

Another key strategy for combating stigma and promoting mental health awareness is to involve individuals with lived experience of mental illness or substance abuse in the planning and delivery of services and support. This may involve establishing peer support programs, hiring individuals with lived experience as staff or consultants, or including them in decision-making processes (Davidson et al., 2012).

Fostering Open Communication and Strong Support Systems

Open communication and strong support systems are essential for promoting mental health and preventing substance abuse. When individuals feel comfortable talking about their thoughts, feelings, and experiences, they are more likely to seek help and support when needed (Vogel et al., 2007).

To foster open communication, it is important to create a safe and non-judgmental environment that encourages self-expression and active listening. This may involve establishing clear boundaries and expectations for communication, practicing empathy and validation, and avoiding criticism or blame (Fava & Sonino, 2000).

It is also important to provide multiple opportunities and channels for communication, such as one-on-one conversations, group discussions, or online forums. This may involve using various communication styles and modalities, such as verbal, written, or creative expression (Pickens, 2012).

Strong support systems are also critical for promoting mental health and preventing substance abuse. Support systems can include family, friends, peers, teachers, healthcare providers, or community organizations (Umberson & Montez, 2010). These support systems can provide emotional support, practical assistance, and a sense of belonging and purpose (Taylor, 2011).

To strengthen support systems, it is important to actively cultivate and maintain positive relationships with others. This may involve setting aside regular time for social activities and interactions, expressing gratitude and appreciation, and providing support and assistance to others when needed (Cacioppo & Cacioppo, 2018).

It is also important to seek out and engage with supportive communities and organizations, such as mental health support groups, recovery communities, or youth programs. These communities can provide a sense of connection, validation, and empowerment, and can offer valuable resources and guidance (White, 2009).

Advocating for Better Access to Mental Health and Addiction Services

Access to mental health and addiction services is a critical component of promoting mental health and preventing substance abuse. However, many individuals face significant barriers to accessing these services, such as lack of insurance coverage, limited availability of services, or stigma and discrimination (Substance Abuse and Mental Health Services Administration, 2019).

To advocate for better access to mental health and addiction services, it is important to raise awareness about the importance of these services and the barriers that individuals face in accessing them. This may involve sharing personal stories and experiences, highlighting the social and economic costs of untreated mental health and substance abuse problems, and calling for policy and system changes (Corrigan & Rao, 2012).

It is also important to engage with policymakers, healthcare providers, and other stakeholders to advocate for increased funding and resources for mental health and addiction services. This may involve participating in advocacy campaigns, attending public hearings or meetings, or joining coalitions or advocacy groups (Satcher & Higginbotham, 2008).

Another key strategy for improving access to mental health and addiction services is to promote the integration of these services into primary care and other healthcare settings. This may involve training primary care providers to screen for and treat mental health and substance abuse problems, establishing collaborative care models that involve mental health and addiction specialists, or using technology to deliver services remotely (Crowley & Kirschner, 2015).

It is also important to advocate for policies and programs that address the social determinants of mental health and substance abuse, such as poverty, housing instability, or trauma. This may involve supporting initiatives that promote economic stability, access to education and job training, or community safety and resilience (Allen et al., 2014).

Conclusion

Progress Made and Gaps That Remain

Over the past several decades, significant progress has been made in understanding and addressing mental health and substance abuse issues among youth. Research has advanced our knowledge of the risk and protective factors that influence mental health and substance use, as well as the effectiveness of various prevention and treatment approaches.

For example, studies have shown that evidence-based prevention programs, such as those that focus on building social-emotional skills or promoting positive family relationships, can significantly reduce the risk of mental health problems and substance abuse among youth (Durlak et al., 2011; National Research Council and Institute of Medicine, 2009). Similarly, research has demonstrated the effectiveness of various treatment approaches, such as cognitive-behavioral therapy and medication-assisted treatment, in helping youth recover from mental health and substance use disorders (Das et al., 2016; Hogue et al., 2018).

In addition to these advances in research, there have also been important policy and practice changes aimed at promoting mental health and preventing substance abuse among youth. For example, the Affordable Care Act has expanded access to mental health and substance abuse services for millions of Americans, including youth (Beronio et al., 2014). Many states and communities have also implemented policies and programs aimed at reducing youth access to alcohol and drugs, such as raising the minimum legal drinking age or implementing prescription drug monitoring programs (Hingson & White, 2014; Pardo, 2017).

However, despite this progress, significant gaps and challenges remain in addressing mental health and substance abuse issues among youth. One major challenge is the persistent stigma surrounding mental health and substance use disorders, which can prevent youth and families from seeking help and support. Studies have shown that negative attitudes and beliefs about mental illness and addiction are still common among both youth and adults, and can act as a barrier to accessing services (Corrigan et al., 2014; Kaushik et al., 2016).

Another challenge is the limited availability and accessibility of mental health and substance abuse services for youth, particularly in certain areas or populations. For example, rural communities often have fewer mental health and substance abuse providers than urban areas, and may face additional barriers such as transportation or financial constraints (Smalley et al., 2010). Similarly, certain groups of youth, such as those from racial or ethnic minority backgrounds or those who identify as LGBTQ+, may face unique challenges in accessing culturally competent and affirming services (Alegria et al., 2010; Marshal et al., 2011).

There are also ongoing concerns about the quality and effectiveness of mental health and substance abuse services for youth. While evidence-based practices have been developed and disseminated, many youth still do not receive care that is consistent with these practices (Garland et al., 2013). Additionally, there are gaps in the workforce and training of mental health and substance abuse professionals, which can limit the availability and quality of services (Hoge et al., 2013).

Finally, there is a need for greater attention to and investment in prevention and early intervention efforts aimed at promoting mental health and preventing substance abuse among youth. While treatment services are critical for those who are already experiencing problems, preventing these problems from developing in the first place can have significant benefits for both individuals and society as a whole. However, funding for prevention programs is often limited, and many communities lack the resources and infrastructure to implement comprehensive prevention efforts (National Research Council and Institute of Medicine, 2009).

The Need for a Comprehensive, Collaborative Approach

To effectively address these ongoing challenges and gaps, it is clear that a comprehensive and collaborative approach is needed. This approach should involve the active engagement and coordination of multiple stakeholders, including parents, schools, healthcare providers, community organizations, policymakers, and youth themselves.

One key element of this approach is the integration of mental health and substance abuse services into other systems and settings where youth spend their time, such as schools and primary care. By providing these services in locations that are easily accessible and familiar to youth, we can reduce barriers to care and improve early identification and intervention (Atkins et al., 2010; Kolko & Perrin, 2014).

Another important element is the development of a skilled and diverse workforce of mental health and substance abuse professionals who are equipped to provide high-quality, culturally responsive services to youth. This may involve increasing funding and support for training programs, as well as implementing strategies to recruit and retain a workforce that reflects the diversity of the youth population (Hoge et al., 2013).

It is also critical to engage and empower youth and families as active partners in promoting mental health and preventing substance abuse. This may involve providing education and resources to help parents and caregivers support the mental health and well-being of their children, as well as creating opportunities for youth to take on leadership roles and advocate for their own health and the health of their peers (Funk et al., 2012; Larson et al., 2005).

Finally, a comprehensive approach to promoting mental health and preventing substance abuse among youth must address the social and environmental factors that influence these issues, such as poverty, trauma, and discrimination. This may involve advocating for policies and programs that promote social and economic equity, as well as supporting community-based initiatives that build resilience and promote positive youth development (Biglan et al., 2012; Yoshikawa et al., 2012).

A Vision for Supporting the Healthy Development of All Youth

Ultimately, the goal of these efforts should be to create a society in which all youth have the opportunity to thrive and reach their full potential. This vision requires a fundamental shift in how we think about and approach mental health and substance abuse issues among youth.

Rather than viewing these issues as individual problems or failures, we must recognize that they are often the result of complex social and environmental factors that shape the lives of youth. By addressing these underlying factors and creating supportive environments that promote resilience and well-being, we can help youth overcome challenges and achieve success in all areas of their lives.

This vision also requires a commitment to equity and social justice, recognizing that certain groups of youth may face unique barriers and challenges that require targeted support and resources. This may include efforts to address the specific needs of youth from diverse racial, ethnic, and cultural backgrounds, as well as those who may be experiencing poverty, homelessness, or other social and economic disadvantages.

Ultimately, supporting the healthy development of all youth requires a long-term investment in prevention, early intervention, and treatment services that are accessible, affordable, and effective. It also requires a willingness to challenge and change the systems and structures that perpetuate inequity and disadvantage, and to create new models of care that are grounded in the values of compassion, collaboration, and community.

Call to Action

Achieving this vision will require the active engagement and commitment of all members of society, including parents, educators, healthcare providers, policymakers, and community leaders. Each of us has a role to play in promoting the mental health and well-being of youth, and in creating a society that supports their healthy development.

For parents and caregivers, this may involve taking an active role in promoting positive family relationships, modeling healthy coping and problem-solving skills, and seeking support and resources when needed. It may also involve advocating for policies and programs that support the mental health and well-being of youth, such as increased funding for school-based mental health services or expanded access to affordable, high-quality childcare.

For educators and school administrators, this may involve implementing evidence-based prevention and early intervention programs, creating positive school climates that promote social and emotional learning, and partnering with mental health and substance abuse providers to ensure that students have access to the services and support they need.

For healthcare providers, this may involve integrating mental health and substance abuse screening and treatment into primary care settings, collaborating with schools and community organizations to provide comprehensive care, and advocating for policies that support the mental health and well-being of youth, such as increased funding for research and workforce development.

For policymakers and community leaders, this may involve championing policies and programs that promote the healthy development of youth, such as investments in early childhood education, affordable housing, and community-based prevention and treatment services. It may also involve working to address the social and economic determinants of health, such as poverty, racism, and discrimination, that can contribute to mental health and substance abuse issues among youth.

Importantly, this call to action also includes youth themselves, who have the power and potential to be leaders and change agents in promoting their own health and well-being and that of their peers. By providing opportunities for youth to take on leadership roles, to have their voices heard, and to be active participants in the decisions that affect their lives, we can empower them to be resilient, engaged, and thriving members of their communities.

Ultimately, promoting the mental health and well-being of youth is not just a matter of addressing individual problems or challenges, but of creating a society that values and supports the healthy development of all young people. By working together across sectors and disciplines, and by leveraging the strengths and assets of youth, families, and communities, we can build a future in which all young people have the opportunity to thrive and achieve their full potential.

This call to action is not just a moral imperative, but an economic and social necessity. The costs of untreated mental health and substance abuse issues among youth are substantial, both in terms of the individual suffering and lost potential, as well as the broader societal costs of healthcare, criminal justice, and lost productivity. By investing in the mental healthand well-being of youth, we can not only improve the lives of individuals and families, but also strengthen the social and economic fabric of our communities and our nation as a whole.

So what can each of us do to answer this call to action and make a difference in the lives of youth? Here are a few suggestions:

1. Educate ourselves and others about mental health and substance abuse issues among youth, and work to reduce the stigma and misconceptions that can prevent youth and families from seeking help.

2. Advocate for policies and programs that support the mental health and well-being of youth, such as increased funding for school-based mental health services, expanded access to affordable and high-quality healthcare, and investments in evidence-based prevention and early intervention programs.

3. Support and participate in community-based efforts to promote positive youth development, such as mentoring programs, after-school activities, and youth leadership initiatives.

4. Model positive coping and problem-solving skills, and create supportive environments that promote resilience and well-being for the youth in our lives, whether as parents, caregivers, educators, coaches, or mentors.

5. Collaborate across sectors and disciplines to provide comprehensive, coordinated care and support for youth and families, and work to build a system of care that is accessible, affordable, and effective for all.

6. Amplify the voices and experiences of youth, and create opportunities for them to be active participants in the decisions that affect their lives and their communities.

7. Invest in research and evaluation to continue to build the evidence base for what works in promoting mental health and preventing substance abuse among youth, and use this evidence to inform policy and practice.

By taking these steps and working together, we can create a society in which all youth have the opportunity to thrive and reach their full potential. It will not be easy, and it will require sustained commitment and effort over time. But the stakes could not be higher, and the potential benefits – for individuals, families, communities, and society as a whole – are immeasurable.

As Nelson Mandela once said, "There can be no keener revelation of a society's soul than the way in which it treats its children." Let us work together to build a society that treats its children with compassion, respect, and dignity, and that invests in their health, well-being, and future success. Let us answer this call to action with courage, conviction, and commitment, and let us not rest until every young person has the opportunity to live a healthy, fulfilling, and productive life.

The time for action is now. The challenges before us are great, but so too are the opportunities. By working together and leveraging the strengths and assets of youth, families, and communities, we can create a brighter future for all. Let us seize this moment and rise to the challenge, for the sake of our youth and for the sake of our shared future.

In conclusion, promoting mental health and preventing substance abuse among youth is not just a public health issue, but a moral and societal imperative. By recognizing the complex social and environmental factors that influence these issues, and by taking a comprehensive, collaborative approach that engages multiple stakeholders and sectors, we can create a society in which all youth have the opportunity to thrive.

This will require investment, commitment, and leadership at all levels – from individuals and families to communities and policymakers. It will require us to challenge the status quo and to imagine new possibilities for how we support and nurture the healthy development of young people.

But the potential rewards are great. By promoting the mental health and well-being of youth, we can not only improve the lives of individuals and families, but also strengthen the social and economic fabric of our communities and our nation as a whole. We can create a society that values and supports the potential of every young person, and that provides them with the resources and opportunities they need to succeed and thrive.

So let us answer this call to action with courage, conviction, and commitment. Let us work together to build a brighter future for all youth, and let us not rest until every young person has the opportunity to live a healthy, fulfilling, and productive life. The time for action is now, and the stakes could not be higher. Let us rise to the challenge, and let us create a society that truly values and supports the healthy development of all its young people.